TIME

A STEP BACKWARD

TIME

A STEP BACKWARD

Eula Collier

iUniverse LLC
Bloomington

Time: A Step Backward

iUniverse books may be ordered through booksellers or by contacting:

iUniverse LLC
1663 Liberty Drive
Bloomington, IN 47403
www.iuniverse.com
1-800-Authors (1-800-288-4677)

ISBN: 978-1-4759-1942-4 (sc)
ISBN: 978-1-4759-1943-1 (e)

Printed in the United States of America

iUniverse rev. date: 03/31/2014

Table of Contents

Acknowledgments

My thanks to the following: Dawn Winn for helping me to get this book started in the right direction; the Morall sisters, Gail and Brenda for helping me along; and my nieces Elaine Webb and Lisa Brooks who finished it.

Remembering Helima Carter (Hoppy), Flora M. Daniels, Annie Hunter (makes a delicious pound cake), Marie Jackson (Marie has a couple of nice books out—look for them), my niece Theodora Higgenbotham, Pamela Wilson, Elder Martie and Donna Deel, Deacon George and Lilly Kimbro, Freddie Bonduraunt, and Anita George (my other daughter). [Inspirations]

Remembering William (first husband and father of my children) died April 4, 1955; Pastor Ephraim and Mary Handley (my parents); son William (Billy) Jr., passed on January 15, 2008. Billy was saved and attended Greater Bethel Church, where the late Elder Byrd Sr. was pastor. He was a great guy and me and my family loved him. All the family loved him. Thank God for his life. My daughter-in-law Florine; my sister Odessa Swafford who passed on November 23, 2010. I loved her dearly. I will always miss her. It's difficult not having her in my life. Her husband, Alburn Swafford, passed January 23, 2004; my second husband, James Collier, passed March 15, 2004. James and Lilly Turner; Mose and Irene Collier; Toni Collier; Will and Neal Kimbro; Elder and Sis. Cora Bohanna; Mary Morall, Evangelist Anita Deel, E. Jordan, Alice Joyce, and Justine Kenard, who was a dynamite cook, whatever she cooked you couldn't stop eating.

Introduction

Time: A Step Backward has been healing for me and a labor of love for my grandchildren, great grandchildren and anyone that would desire to experience and understand family life on Paint Creek during the 1930s in southwestern West Virginia. Paint Creek is one of many historical sites in West Virginia. This winding body of water would take you from one small town to the next. Our family lived in Milburn, one of several coalmining communities located along Paint Creek. While the community of Milburn no longer exists and the mines have long since closed, Paint Creek continues to flow through the mountains of West Virginia. Milburn holds many fond memories for me. It was here that I learned about love, life and the true light.

This book will give you a glimpse into the family life of an African-American family living in a small segregated coalmining community in rural West Virginia. You will be encouraged to know that if I can make it through the trials and tribulations of life during this era then you too can make it through your life challenges.

1

The Way It Was

Year: 1936

I grew up in the coalmining community of Milburn, West Virginia. Milburn was one of many such communities located along Paint Creek in the southwestern part of West Virginia.

The history of Paint Creek goes back to pioneer times. It was the site of an early Native American trail that led from the Shawnee villages on the Scioto River in Ohio to the east. This trail followed the Kanawha River crossing it below Paint Creek located in West Virginia and then continued its course for several miles along Paint Creek. Once the early travelers reached the present day Long Branch (small community along Paint Creek), they stripped the bark from nearby trees and painted them red. Paint Creek, as evidenced by early records, took its name from the painted trees that stood near its banks. Local historians report that Native Americans gathered here prior to their raids into Greenbrier County, West Virginia; it was definitely a stopping place on their return to their villages.

Up until the mid 1800s the Paint Creek area was primarily agricultural, with its early residents depending upon the land and the forests for their livelihood. However, this would soon change; the first industrial development would begin around 1853.

My dad was a minister and a coal miner. He was short of stature yet a man of integrity. He loved God and he loved his family. We knew that he meant what he said and said what he meant. Dad didn't believe in repeating himself. He was respected in our home and in the community.

Dad served as pastor of Milburn Baptist Church and later became the pastor of the Mahan Baptist Church. I never knew him to have an altercation with anyone.

Mom was a quiet, God-fearing woman who loved going to church. She spent her time cooking, canning, baking, sewing and making our house a home. She taught my sisters and me to do the same. Mom was known for her hospitality and people loved her because they could always count on her to be the same kind person each time they were in her presence.

In our family there was my older brother, Ephriam, who got sick and died from influenza as a teenager; three older sisters: Geneva, Nellie and Bertha who left home while I was young; my younger sister Gertrude, who passed at a young age; Odessa my youngest sister and my niece Thelma who lived with us while her mother worked in Pittsburgh. I am currently the only surviving member of the family.

As children, if we wanted to go somewhere special we would start asking dad early on to give him time to make up his mind. He would want to know, where we were going, how we were getting there and who we were going with. Mom would often intervene on our behalf.

Growing up in West Virginia wasn't bad for me. We lived there and that was that. We were aware of what was happening within the community and we loved the part of life that we were involved in. We went to school, church, and the movies. We did what we were told to do and not what we wanted to do.

We also had many fun times living in Milburn. We would climb the hills and mountains looking for nuts in the fall, swing on vines across the creek, swim and fish. Someone once yelled bear while we were in the mountains and I began to run and did not look back until I was almost home. I never stopped to confirm if it was true. I don't think there really was a bear but you never know and I was not taking any chances on there being a bear.

Some of the children would laugh and make fun of other children. I have seen them do it. I wondered why because each family had the same thing, nothing. What little they had they needed. I do not ever remember making fun of anyone. No one had to tell me that, even at an early age, I was sensitive toward anyone that had problems of any kind.

I attended a one-room school from the first to the sixth grade. There was no space for expansion. My school was also where we attended church. We had one teacher for the entire school, Ms. Mary McKinney. Our school had about 25 students. The schools in those days were segregated; black and white children did not attend school together.

We were in school from 9:00 a.m. to 3:00 p.m. Monday through Friday. I would eat my lunch at home. Prayer service was held on Wednesday nights at 7:30 p.m. and on Sunday there was Sunday school, and morning service. There was even night service on some Sundays.

I never skipped school, not that I wanted to. The school/church was close to home. In fact, I could hear the school bell ring from my house and still have time to get to school before class started. In my family, you went to church and school. No excuses or exceptions unless you were sick, and if you were sick, you didn't go out to play that day.

My younger sister Odessa and I would fight when our parents were not around. I was bigger and older but she was always ready to fight. I would hit her and run behind closed doors to get away from her. She was very aggressive and would try to knock the door down. I loved my sister and will always miss her. If we were caught fighting both of us would get a whipping. We were not allowed to fight each other so neither of us would tell our parents about our fights.

Odessa and I would often laugh about how we were not allowed to iron and do household chores on Sunday. We would slip the iron into our room to iron something we wanted to wear to church. Our parents taught us that we had six days to do these chores and Sundays were reserved for church and rest. The only chore allowed was cleaning the dishes after eating.

My dad was injured in the mines when he was around 45 years old. Although he was a relatively young man, he was never able to work in the coalmines again. After several years of going to different doctors and taking many tests, he was finally compensated for his injuries and put on disability. I thank the Lord he received his disability compensation in his lifetime. He told his family that if something happened to him, we should not pursue it, but I would have.

Every other weekend dad would sell fish. He would order it through the company store, and pick it up on Friday afternoon. I was about nine years old at this time and big enough to bring the wagon to help him with deliveries. It was fun for me at the time. There were houses all along the way to the store. Dad was an industrious man and always found a way to bring income into the house. He was also a successful minister and often received invitations to preach up and down Paint Creek.

Although I didn't grow up on a farm, we raised hogs and chickens and grew our own vegetables. I helped in the garden, by dropping seeds and setting out plants. I didn't mind feeding the chickens, but I never wanted to be bothered with hogs. My other job outside was pulling weeds. Everyone in the household had chores to do. I would clean my own room, and help to clean the rest of the house. My mom would bake a large cake each week that I would often share with my friends. All of my friends wanted a slice of mom's cake.

I recall when I was about eleven and eating a peach I decided to plant the peach seed in our front yard. In fact, the tree grew up with me and I would take care of it. The tree bore beautiful peaches and I remember making my first peach pie.

On Sunday morning, between Sunday school and church, we had a half hour break and the children would go to the poolroom to purchase snacks. The poolroom was located a short distance from the church. We would buy sodas, candy, popcorn, and ice cream.

There was a fall festival at the church once a year. We played games and there was food for sale. The children enjoyed participating in a game called bobbing for apples. The object was to grab an apple without using your hands. It is not an easy thing to do, but some of us did succeed at doing so. It was a lot of fun.

One of the ministers at our church didn't have a car. He would walk from Long Branch to Milburn, about five miles one-way. When I think about his dedication and commitment I marvel because he rarely ever missed a service.

When a guest minister ran revival at our church, certain members would take turns inviting him and the pastor to dinner. We always took our turn in having the guest minister over for dinner. Guest ministers would stay at one of the deacon's houses. The revival meeting would last a week at a time. My mom would bake a cake or pie, fry chicken, have a fresh vegetable; usually greens or green beans, potato salad and homemade bread.

I never had to wait for the guest minister to eat, but some children did, my mom always let me eat when the food was ready. If I needed a refill of something I would go back to the kitchen, there was no problem. We always had plenty of good food.

Reflections

At Christmas time, the coal company would give the miners gifts such as turkeys, candy, fruit and nuts. We had a nice dinner on all holidays. As a matter of fact, we had good food most of the time. The neighborhood boys would come around selling Christmas trees. Almost all the neighbors, had trees, especially the ones with children. It was a joy to see children running in and out of their houses while the Christmas lights, were shining through the windows, day and night. Since electricity didn't cost much at this time. This scene would be repeated up and down Paint Creek.

My friend May and I would regularly go to the poolroom during the weekday to purchase candy and other snacks. It seemed that whenever we walked into the building there would be music playing on the jukebox and May and I would start dancing. I believe that the manager enjoyed our dancing and would play the music when he saw us approaching. They were entertained and so were we.

One of my friends in the neighborhood had a record player at her house, so we would go to her house to listen to music. They had one of the latest ones made. The one my mom had was a tabletop, but you had to keep working with it to get it to play. I didn't bother with it very much, mom had it every since I could remember.

Friends were valuable and when you found a friend you almost always had a friend for life. Yet, everyone was not a friend. There were many acquaintances. Jolene was just such a person. Jolene and I were classmates throughout middle school. When I didn't go home for lunch, I would offer her some of my lunch and she would always accept.

One day, Jolene came to school, and announced that she was going home with me for dinner. I will never forget it; dinner that evening was cabbage, corn bread, liver with onions and gravy and apple pie. Jolene refused dinner because she did not eat liver. Fortunately for her, the carnival happened to be nearby and we decided to go and I bought her a couple of hot dogs.

When I was about eleven years old I was invited to be part of a singing group. Mrs. Chambers of Kingston, a well known woman in the Paint Creek area, would pick me and three other children up on Friday evening, and bring us back home on Sunday. This was mostly in the summer when we were not in school. We would go to different churches and sing. Two of us were from Milburn, and the other two were from Kingston. Mrs. Chambers would speak and we would sing with all our might.

Mega was a pal of mine. Her mom and stepfather made an alcohol drink that we called "home made brew." Mega would sneak a couple jars from her parents' stash and we would go down by the creek and drink and swim. We made sure that we were in a place where no one could see us. I always had my limit, because I couldn't go home drunk or even smell of the stuff. I had never seen my father or mother drink and I knew they would not tolerate me doing so.

Although my father was a minister, my sisters made their own choices when they became adults. Sometimes those choices were contrary to how they were raised. My sister Nellie would have me go to a neighbor's house with a note requesting a pint of liquor on credit until her paycheck. I made these runs for my sister (without my father's knowledge) until one day I just got tired of doing this and yelled aloud from the middle of the road: "does anyone want a drink of liquor?". I was only kidding, but my sister got wind of it and did not take it as a joke. To my delight, that was the end of my liquor runs.

Sister Geneva didn't smoke but she once had a toothache so bad that she tried smoking a pipe for relief. After a few days Geneva was forced to go to the dentist. The dentist was a smart guy, but he loved to drink. Geneva also decided to have a drink along with the dentist to kill the pain. She woke up the next day still in pain. We discovered that the dentist had pulled the wrong tooth. She went back the following day to have the right tooth pulled. The moral of this story is that if the dentist is drinking don't drink with him and be sure to not let him work in your mouth.

My sister Bertha was married to Joseph. Joseph never wanted to listen to other people. He once had a wreck while driving his tractor and injured his foot and leg. He was blessed to get out alive but he developed a limp from the accident that remained with him the rest of his life because he never wanted to use crutches or a cane. Bertha and Joseph had no children, so she was very happy for me to spend time with them. Their house was also convenient for me to get to school when I started high school.

January 1938 was a fairly normal winter day and evening when we retired for the night. The snow had just begun to fall. When daylight came I immediately wondered why my mom had not called me to get up for school. When I peered out the window, I didn't want to believe what I saw.

There was so much snow, no cars were running, and there were no lights anywhere. The heavy blanket of snow remained for about a week before the roads were cleared, and the miners were finally returned to work and we could go back to school. We used oil lamps in lieu of electricity.

On Wednesday nights we were normally in prayer service. The person speaking that evening was teaching the youth how to pray. We were called on one at a time to pray. One of the guys, John, would write his prayer, and read it without people knowing he was reading. Consequently, church members would brag about how John could really pray, but they never knew he was reading his prayer. One day John had turned my name in to the principal along with a few other students for misbehaving on the school bus. On this particular Wednesday as he began to pray, I reached over and took the paper he was reading from. When I did this, he began repeating the same phrases until he decided to end the prayer. It wasn't a nice thing to do, but the payback felt good.

One Wednesday night, I didn't go to the prayer service. I was home doing homework and my older sister Nellie was with me. Her boyfriend James came by. He knew my dad was at church. James was upset about something and started an argument. That was not allowed in our house. He began to get loud. I looked up and he had a gun. At that point, I simply forgot I was afraid of the dark even though there were lights where I had to go, and I ran all the way to the church and told my dad that James was in our house with a gun. Dad jumped up and ran out of the church immediately. Our house was only a few minutes way from the church.

When we arrived home, James was still there, because he didn't know I was gone, or that I had seen the gun. My dad confronted him. He lied and said he never had a gun, and that he would not disrespect our home in that manner. My dad asked him to leave, and never come back. Thank God there was no problem. James had a reputation for being rude and obnoxious but this time he had gone to far.

Plans Not Carried Out

One of my jobs as a child included bringing in the wood for the household before night. The houses were built high enough up from the ground that you could store the wood under the house and it would not get wet from the rain, snow, or other elements.

I was about eight years old and as was my habit, I went under the house to get firewood that my dad had chopped and to my surprise, a friend of my dad's was there when I arrived. It was one way in and one way out. Once you are under the porch you had to step inside the door where the wood was. The first thing that came to my mind was why was he there and how did he get under there without being seen. He whispered come on in, you know me. Of course, I knew him, he would come to our house but I was stunned to see him under the house. He said he wanted to play a game in the dark. It was about 8:00 p.m., almost dark.

I almost didn't believe what was happening, I did not know a thing about playing a game in the dark. He said sit down, I have some money for you. I said you know I am not allowed to accept money. He said take it, I will tell your dad. I did not know at that time but he really had nerve. He gave me a dollar, I gave it back. I told him that was not enough money for my buddy and me. He was already on his knees, because you could not stand up under the porch. Being on his knees made him about the same height as me. He reached for my hand as if he was going to dance. He kind of stumbled and his hand missed mine and hit my leg. In the meantime, he was trying to kiss me. That never happened either.

I said I have to go and I left. He said come back tomorrow and I will have $5 for you and your buddy. The next evening, I went back under the house but I was not alone, I had my buddy stand on the side so he could not see her. The minute I opened the door, he was there and said here is your money, I will tell your dad about it. (I really don't remember him giving me money in my dad's presence at any other time.) I took the money and said here is my buddy, maybe she will play your game in the dark. He whispered, no, no, go, go.

I should have told my parents or an adult about the incident. When you find yourself in such a position you need to tell someone what is happening. Otherwise, they cannot help you.

An incident somewhat similar occurred when May and I were playing near the creek and a strange man came up to us and offered to pay us a nickel if we would lay down on a nearby rock. He did not say what we had to do after that but we did not stick around to find out. We took off running toward home. We did not see the man again.

2

Paint Creek: The Community

Kingston was the closest community to Milburn. It was also a coal mining community with its own company store, post office and schools. Anytime you went to Kingston there was the smell of fresh fish frying. The residents loved fried fish and it was an inexpensive meal.

Dr. Pope was the closest doctor and he lived in Kingston, and cared for three communities. He was only in his office during weekday afternoons from 2:30 p.m.-5:00 p.m. Neighbors who owned cars willingly took you to the doctor's office. They would be glad to make the trip to get gas money or extra cash for their pocket.

If you were sick there were grey pills for pain, and sulfa drugs for colds, fever, pneumonia, and any other infection. Every family had these pills, and they really worked. If there was an emergency, and someone was around with a car, they would take you to the hospital. People mostly depended on the two pills. If anyone was out of pills, it was no big deal, because all the neighbors had them. Dr. Pope would give you a small envelope consisting of about a dozen pills and when you ran out you could always go back for more. He kept them in a big jar. Whoever made it to his office while he was there, was in luck.

Because there was only one doctor, we would often have to take care of our own ailments. One time while walking barefooted, I stepped on a rusty nail. It was the weekend, so my dad poured turpentine on it and wrapped it up. It was swollen and discolored. The doctor was not around. I went to him on Monday and he gave me a shot and my foot got better as time went by. I hopped around about a week on crutches. I never walked outside without my shoes again.

The most exciting thing that happened in Kingston was the annual carnival. Most residents that had transportation would go to the carnival. The carnival would last one or two weeks. Most residents around Paint Creek would go to the carnival.

The next small town was Westerly. In Westerly there was a small company store, post office and a one-room school. Black folks lived mostly on the side of the hill in Westerly, and the whites lived near the highway. Though the houses in Westerly were on a fairly steep hill, they were in better condition than homes in some of the other communities. A few black families lived on the lower part of the hill, but were still segregated.

Krebs Community was about two miles from Milburn. Krebs was the opposite direction from Westerly. We had friends there and would walk to visit them. We walked everywhere we went, so we stayed pretty healthy.

Those that had transportation went to the Gallagher community theatre. They had the best movies. There were two shows a night but we always went to the first movie so we could make it home before dad's curfew. The Gallagher theatre had popcorn and other snacks to purchase.

Segregation was the law at this time therefore blacks had a school and whites had a school. Black and white children would talk to each other but we did not play together. Every school year my teacher, Ms. McKinney, would have the students sell candy for the school. The white neighbors usually bought candy from us, but very few blacks. I would also sell Cloverine Ointment—a popular ointment used for sores, insect bites, and other skin problems.

There were only two theaters in the eleven small communities along Paint Creek. People would come from surrounding communities to go to the theater. The neighborhood children in Milburn would walk to the theater since it was located only about a miles away for most residents.

At the theatre, blacks sat on the left side in the middle. They had about six rows, eight seats in a row. Whites sat in front of the theater. The adult whites would normally sit in the back of the theater and white children in the front. On the right side of the theater it was white only. Very few black adults went to the movies.

One Sunday afternoon, after coming home from church, my friends and I decided to go to the local theatre wearing our Sunday clothes. It appeared that the white children resented the idea, that we had something nice to wear. Two girls and one boy tried to block the entrance, and asked, "Did you all rob a store?" We kept walking toward them. We never backed down so they let us pass. We had them outnumbered. They thought we were going to fight, but none of us wanted trouble, but they didn't know this. We kept walking toward them and they eventually moved out of our way. This was such an uncomfortable experience that we decided not to go to the movies on Sunday again.

Milburn had one dirt road that ran through the entire community with houses on both sides for about a half-mile. Rain or snow it was muddy and on hot dry days it was dusty. On the wet days one needed boots even if you walked close to the fences of the houses to keep from getting your shoes dirty. The worst area was called the "bottom." This is where the potholes were deeper, wider, and more difficult to navigate when it rained or snowed.

Our house was located on a hill and it wasn't far from the railroad tracks. One day we were just standing on the bridge where the freight train that carried the coal cars passed by when the guys that were operating the train threw us a bag of candy and this started a routine for us. We would be waiting for the train, every other day to get candy. This lasted until they changed employees and no more candy.

In Milburn, we had to walk pass the white community to get to the store. If we walked the railroad tracks we could avoid passing through this part of the community. We often walked the railroad when going to the store. The next towns were Mahan, Collinsdale, Sandy City, Burnwell, Whitaker, Standard, and then Gallagher. Most of the communities were set up similar to Milburn. If they were smaller and some were, they would not have a company store and would go to the store nearest them. There was no coalmine in Gallagher or Standard. In Mahan someone would get shot just about every Saturday night.

Milburn was divided into several sections. There was the tipple where the miners entered the coalmines. They rode into the mine [the mine in Milburn was on the side of a hill] on trolley cars. The cars would take them straight up the mountain and into the coal mine.

Close to the Tipple were about ten double houses; four rooms on each side. One person would rent one side and another the other side. The rent was taken out of the miner's payroll check before the miner saw it. Black people lived there. At the end of the housing complex was a white lady that rented a double house and had tenants that didn't speak English.

A cement building was nearby. This building was always kept locked, because it contained dynamite and other explosives used for mining. You had to have a written order from one of the mining officials to enter the building.

The next section of housing was called "Hunk Hill." The houses were built on the side of a hill and this is where the majority of the white community lived.

A short distance from Hunk Hill was the main section of Milburn. This is where one would find the doctor's office, theatre, company store, post office, homes of the mine supervisors and the local sheriff.

There was one sheriff for three communities. Whenever there was a serious issue, the sheriff would call for back up from the sheriff in the next community which was about five or six miles away.

If you needed something from the store there was the "company store". The company store was owned and operated by the mining company. It was open five days a week, and a half a day on Saturday. The store was closed from Saturday afternoon until 8:00 a.m. Monday morning. Coal miners were able to purchase groceries and other items on credit until payday. Thus came the phrase "I owe my soul to the company store." For many families this was a reality.

One had to work for the Milburn Colliery Company (the Company) to rent a house in Milburn. Everybody rented from the Company. There was one black man that worked at the store and not inside of the mines; his name was Bart, he also delivered groceries. A white man drove the truck, and Bart did the deliveries. The white guy would help if necessary. Whatever you ordered at the store, the Company would deliver.

Twice a week, the company store would dispose of food that they could not sell. The workers would load the food in the truck and dump it with the other trash. The place they dumped it was called the trash pile. I noticed people going to it because it was just below our house. Different ones would go when they saw the truck because some of the food, such as the fruit, bread, and even some meat was edible. The ones that got the food were not ashamed. Some adults would send their children. I know for a fact that they would eat this food. It was probably okay before they dumped it with the trash. I wondered why the company store chose not to give the food away.

The graveyard for blacks was a short distance from the church. Space was cleared for this purpose. You didn't have to buy the land. The gravediggers would put family members together. Every now and then, someone would bury a loved one in Beckley, W.Va., about nineteen miles away. Most likely they had family nearby.

Only certain residents in Milburn had telephones: the sheriff, store manager, general manager of the coal mines, the guy that ran the movie theatre, the post office clerk, and a family that would cash your script for twenty five cents off a dollar. When you went to the company store and you needed money, the office would advance you coins that were called "scrip". If you had five dollars in scrip you would receive about $3.75 cash. If you needed cash for an emergency you could go to the company store and draw an advance on your paycheck.

In 1939, the first television arrived in Milburn. The television belonged to Ms. Jackson, a black woman, known for her hospitality would allow neighborhood children to gather at her house; black and white, to watch. Children would be all over the porch and as many as could be would be inside. The black and white TV had a small screen with an antenna, and the reception was not great but it was something to look at and we were amazed.

The fourth of July was a great time for us. Most of the families in the community purchased ice cream from the company store. It came in five-gallon containers. The flavors were vanilla, strawberry and chocolate. There was always lots of ice cream during this time. We would go to each other's house and eat ice cream. The neighbors that didn't have children did not have to buy ice cream because there was plenty to go around for anyone that wanted some. There was also lots of good food around. The Fourth was a special time for the residents of Paint Creek.

Another fun day was the annual United Mine Workers Local Union celebration, which occurred on the first Saturday in September. This event drew large crowds from people all along Paint Creek. There would be a huge picnic and other fun activities going on.

3

The Neighbors on Paint Creek

I would often go to the company store. If a neighbor saw me going and requested that I pick up something for them I would gladly do so. However, if that neighbor did not bother to tip me for my service I would purposely go a different route since they did not appreciate my service.

One afternoon I went to the store alone and ran into a white girl around my age that had a reputation for being a bully. She bumped into me on purpose and this started a fight between us outside of the store. I believe that I hit her harder than she expected and she quickly disappeared from the scene. I left the store and walked home using the railroad tracks because we could go either way. This girl had two sisters who were older and bigger than me. I soon noticed that they were trying to cross the creek to get to me. There was a way you had to cross the creek, by jumping from one rock to another. I began to run down the tracks toward home. It took time and skill to cross the creek and the girls never caught up with me. I ran all the way home. My sister saw me coming from a distance and said stop running! I looked around and there was no one behind me so I had outrun them.

After that incident, I would only go to the store with friends. If there was more than one, the white children wouldn't bother you. I didn't fear them. In fact, none of us did. We were not around one another that often. The only place we were together at the same time was the theatre, and we did not sit together. We came out at the same time, but everyone went their separate way. We had two different directions to go so it wasn't crowded.

A couple of friends and I were hanging out when we noticed a neighbor; Rena and her five children. The children looked to be from 3 to 7 years of age. We knew Rena had children but I had never seen them all at once. The children ran in and out of neighbors' yards and were literally all over the road. They were headed to the poolroom. My friends and I decided to follow them to just observe. As soon as they arrived at the pool room a couple of the young ones started yelling for ice cream. They were all over the place and Rena could not keep up with them. I wondered why she did not leave half of them at home with her husband. They knocked over everything they could reach. They were inside the poolroom for 8 to 10 minutes if that long. As soon as they were served the store attendant helped Rena to get them out of the store and on her way.

We followed Rena and the children all the way home to her house. I had never seen children so out of control. The whole experience was funnier than going to the movies.

In the summer, my friend May and I would go to the hills close by the house and get spring water as it flowed down the rocks. We also enjoyed swinging on the grapevines over the creek. God took care of us. There was no TV or telephone, just radio in our homes. I did enjoy reading thou and spent a lot of time doing so.

As a teenager, just about all the children in my age group were learning to smoke. I tried to smoke but could never inhale properly and would get strangled. I now thank God that I was unsuccessful in my efforts to smoke. It meant that I didn't have to quit. Smoke and air are similar in that they cannot be bottled up. Both keep moving and get into everything. We now know that only the fresh air is good for you.

In each community there was a small place where young people gathered to socialize. This place was called a juke joint. There would be a nickel machine that played records; and you could purchase sodas, chips, and candy. When the records changed, about every two weeks, there would be free record playing and some of us would go over in the early evening and dance.

There was a deacon, and his wife, that lived on one side of us, that attended our church named the Hastings. They asked my mom if I could sleep over at their house at night. Her husband worked the midnight shift. I supposed she was just nervous. I would go over before dark, and would be asleep when he went to work. I was over their house one afternoon and she sent me to pick up her mail at the post office. To get your mail, you walked or rode to the post office and asked for it. No one brought it to you.

Voting took place in the white school. This was the only time that blacks saw the inside of the building. Volunteers would be available to offer a ride to the polls and back home. Some blacks would accept a ride even though it was in walking distance. When the weather was bad those same folks offering rides wouldn't stop to help people, even if they were carrying groceries and obviously needed a ride.

I knew a girl whose mother went to vote. She was walking to the polls alone at dusk. She noticed a car parked where she had to pass and suddenly became fearful. This was no place for a car and there were two men inside the car. The lady started calling out for a neighbor that lived on the corner, and running as she called. The guys in the car looked at her but made no attempt to bother her. Nothing happened that evening and finally, a friend showed up and the two ended up going to the voting booth together. A rather scary evening that ended just fine.

On one beautiful summer evening some neighbors not too far from our home gave their only daughter an elaborate wedding. The Hayfields had two sons and one daughter. We stood on the bridge across the road from their house. Both white and blacks watched the wedding. It was on the porch of their rather large home. Guests were all over the yard and everyone was dressed in their finest. The bride was beautiful and a genuinely nice person. The bride acknowledged the onlookers with a wave and smile. She probably would have given us a piece of cake were it not for her friends. It was a memorable event in our neighborhood.

Neighborhood Drama

One time the sheriff arrested a black man by the name of Dex for being drunk and disorderly. Dex was in his 30s and small of stature for a grown man. I don't know how, but Dex took the sheriff's gun away from the him during the arrest. Fortunately, no one was hurt. Eventually, the sheriff got his gun back from Dex; who was arrested and taken off to jail. I wasn't around when this incident occurred but it was the talk of the town.

The Robins family moved in our neighborhood and was quickly known for their card parties, and their nickel music machine. They could get quite noisy on the weekends, but they had to keep it down, because the Company would evict them in a heartbeat. One day Mr. Robins had a problem with one of his customers, there was a fight and Mr. Robins took a butcher knife and cut the customer's throat. The body was there all day because the sheriff was out of town. Some of the kids would go in to see him. His body was on the floor until the sheriff arrived and called another sheriff for back up before the ambulance came. There were no 911 services to call, and the deputy sheriff was five miles away. Mr. Robins was eventually taken to jail, and because he had nowhere to run. He just waited for the police. His wife also arrived. They lived about a mile away from where the incident occurred. At that time, if the man of the house was not working in the mines, the family had to give up the house. The prospects were not good for Mrs. Robins to remain in Milburn.

There were a couple of neighbors that managed to make extra money from their homes. Ms. Rose as we called her sold food and alcohol from her home. She also had a nickel machine that she kept on and turned up so she attracted a good bit of attention. Ms. Rose lived fairly close to our home and would not allow her music to be too loud when my dad was home. She knew he was a minister, and she respected him. Another business woman was Mrs. Mason, who lived about a mile from our house and was known to make the best hot dogs on Paint Creek. She only sold the hot dogs on the weekend and blacks and whites bought them as fast as she could make them. She sold out every weekend. People would drive miles just to get one of Mrs. Mason's hot dogs.

It was quite common during this time for people to buy excess liquor from the state run liquor stores and then sell it for profit out of their homes. There was a neighbor in our community who had such a business. This of course was illegal, even though most people in the community knew about it. The interesting thing was that blacks attempting this business were often raided by the police soon after starting. On the other hand, whites were able to maintain their home businesses without interference by the police.

Some of the men would get drunk on payday and beat their wives. It didn't matter if they were pregnant or not. Others demonstrated even more bizarre behavior. One such example is Mr. Genson who was known to lock his wife in the house and nail down the windows when he went to work. People called it jealous. I could think of some other things to call it. The Gensons had no children even though he treated her like a child. Mrs. Genson wasn't allowed to go anywhere, or talk to anyone without him. He soon left the area where people knew him. When they left her eyes were really black and blue. Whenever her black eye cleared up, he would give her another one.

Robb and Rose enjoyed having a drink in the evenings but Rose always drank too much. One day she got drunk, and her husband was about to discipline her child (by another relationship). Rose got between Robb and the child and stabbed him to death. A couple of weeks before, Robb's cousin killed a nun, because he had just come out of a halfway house and wanted drugs. After he killed her he hid her body behind a relative's house. He was using the nun's telephone. That's how they caught him.

Ms. Deanna ran a boarding house and I would wash dishes for her some evenings after school. I had washed dishes for about two weeks, and it was time for her to pay me. She made up some silly excuse, and did not give me my money. Ms. Deanna loved to drink alcohol, which she did most days, and she was too sick, or should I say too hung over to think straight. I didn't say anything. I just walked out and went home, because I couldn't tell her what I wanted to say. There was a ballgame on Saturday. Her husband was the manager of the team and all the kids rode in a stand up truck. We would pay $1.25 each for the ride. She didn't even pay my way to the game. I asked her for my money again and she made up an excuse as to why she could not pay me. In a very nice way, I asked her if she wanted me to continue to do the dishes? She said, yes. "I just looked at her, and walked away, this time for good."

Ms. Deanna had boarders, and her husband worked in the coalmines, so she had extra cash. She finally stopped asking me to work because I never showed up for duty. I was a teenager and was looking forward to the extra change, but I refused to work for free.

Most of the men in the neighborhood worked in the mines—either Milburn or Mahan. There would be a truck that went from house to house picking them up. A few had to go out of Paint Creek to plants about twenty miles away, that's what Paint Creek was all about. The men would travel from one community to another doing what they had to do to survive. Some worked on the railroad and did odd jobs like working in local stores keeping the shelves stocked, cutting grass, and cleaning up the place.

Mr. Jake worked in a nearby grocery store. Every other Wednesday he would come to Milburn and take your grocery orders and bring them back on Friday. My mom and dad usually purchased flour, meal, coffee, and any dry goods, that they needed.

I remember my dad would pay him when he brought the food because he didn't want any bills. The guy drove a big truck and made many deliveries. He was always by himself. He would come as far as Milburn, and turn around and head back to Montgomery. As I think back, I wonder why he never had help. He wasn't in any hurry because I guess the more time he took to get the job done, the more money he made.

Mrs. Myers lived just outside of Milburn. She wasn't able to get around on her own. She needed help. Mrs. Myers kept boarders in her house. The only thing she did was give orders, and collect money that she wasn't able to spend.

Mrs. Myers was known to be mean. She was mean to those who came to help her with housework. She was even mean to her husband. She would yell and scream about something all the time. She treated him like a disobedient child or worse. A dear friend of mine named Berea lived with her a short time and went to school. Mrs. Myers, was trying to keep her there until she was old enough to marry Mrs. Myers' brother.

She wouldn't let Berea take piano lessons, right there in their house. Her husband took out insurance on another man, because he drank all the time, but Mrs. Myers' husband died first and never got a chance to collect. He was a drunk himself. At that time the men who drank alcohol would drink and stumble up and down the highway. Nobody cared, and no one was around to arrest them. It was just a way of life. It was rare to see a woman in this condition.

One Sunday morning we were coming from the poolroom on our way back to church, and we had to pass by the front of the company store when we noticed a man lying face down on the ground below us, a neighbor named Patrick. Patrick was often drunk and apparently he stumbled and fell head first over the railing. Had he turned and walked straight, someone would have seen him. There was no investigation of Patrick's death because no one thought it was foul play.

No one knew how long Patrick had been dead. The store had been closed twenty-four hours, and I wondered why he was in that area. The sheriff called for the assistance of a neighboring sheriff before they moved him. At that time anyone that needed the sheriff would simply go to his house and knock on the door. There were few telephones in the neighborhood. Those that had telephones would willingly make calls for you in an emergency, or anytime. If you needed the doctor after hours, it was the same. People in the community were helpful to one another.

My dad and Mr. Myers worked together in the mines. As far as I knew he was a nice man. When things didn't go well for him in the mines, like a shovel handle breaking or something going wrong with the coal cars in the mines while working—he would refrain from using bad language because he knew my dad was a minister.

Some of the miners lived in one community and worked in another. Wherever the miners worked, transportation was provided for them usually in the form of a truck that would go around and pick them up early in the mornings.

I knew a lady that kept two boys and a girl. The children were afraid of her. I saw her beat them quite a bit. If neighbors passed by she didn't stop. I suppose because the children were not related to her. She was always abusing them. It was so sad because they were around eight and nine years old.

No one bothered to speak to her about her behavior that I know of but she would have the children working excessively. I felt so sad for them. When they left Paint Creek and I often thought about them and wondered if anyone ever took them away from her. She lived in Gallagher and one of my school buddies would see them all the time.

She would send them to Sunday School and church. Even though she didn't go herself. When the Baptist Convention was held at the Gallagher church, I often served as the delegate. I was about fifteen years old. They were there and I suppose that's the only time they felt free. They were not allowed to go to school functions or movies.

I only saw them at school or church. They never played ball or anything. They lived in fear. Whenever she called them, they would run. Just the sound of her voice would frighten them. I often wandered what happened to the children.

This same lady had a younger guy to come to her house because she took in boarders. Later on she found out that he was sick, but she never found out what was wrong with him. He wanted to run the numbers, but didn't know how. This guy didn't know anything about the numbers racket. He was trying to do what another guy was doing. I don't remember anyone getting caught. Like everything else, no one complained. There was no one to enforce the law, but the sheriff, and he didn't bother about that, because he felt he had more important things to do. This guy wanted a job in the coalmines at least he thought he did. He grew up in the mining town, and went away to college. He decided to quit school, and come back to Milburn to work in the coalmines, not realizing that mining is the hardest, and probably one of the most dangerous jobs there is. The miners had no choice. There were no other jobs close around where we lived.

The Sherwood family consisted of a mother, her daughter Myra, son Brad. The mother and son (young adult) loved to gamble. Brad was shot and killed at the gambling table. The mother had a boyfriend, that she was trying to get rid of, but was unable to break the relationship off. He wouldn't take no for an answer, so in the midst of a family dispute—he shot her, and she died. Myra was left to live with an aunt that wasn't very nice. You're blessed, when you live, to be able to raise your own children.

Fred, who was married and living on Paint Creek was known to be fooling around with his neighbor's wife and most everyone knew about it. The affair had gone on for about a month.

The woman Fred was sneaking around with was married to Ed. Ed apparently got wind of what was going on and started following the two of them. One day he caught Fred out alone and shot him. The news got around fast. Fred was left to die on the road where he was shot. By the time he was discovered laying on the pavement it was too late for help.

People that lived nearby knew what Fred was up to. They were not hiding their relationship and everyone was talking but it never stopped them until tragedy struck. Ed let his wife live but he still had to spend time in prison.

Another story often talked about was a few young adults that were on their way to get hot dogs when two other cars had the road blocked talking. The drivers of the two cars blocking the roadway refused to pull over out of the main roadway. The man that wanted to get by was rather hot headed and pulled out a gun and made everybody get out but the driver because he had to move the car. The guy shot up in the air to show he was serious about his request.

By that time, another car arrives on the scene and the guy in the third car carried a knife. Can you imagine someone with a knife going up against a gun, but I have been told he hit everything he aimed at. The guy with the gun kept running his mouth at the guy with the knife, and threatening him. The guy threw the knife, and hit him in the arm as he held the gun. He wasn't trying to kill him but what a way to get one's attention. The gunman needed medical attention and had to be taken to the doctor's office. Fortunately for him the doctor was in his office. The police was called and eventually showed up but the case was dropped because everyone had a different story about the event.

A white couple living in Gallagher with three young boys were on their way home from the hospital with a new baby girl and the word was that her husband got angry at his wife on the way home from the hospital and stopped and put her out of the car. She was walking along the road when another neighbor passed by that knew her, and was wondering what the trouble was. Her husband replied she got out of the car for air. At that time, he pretended to persuade his wife to get in the car because he didn't want people talking.

The next car that approached the family was a man that knew them. He lived in Gallagher and was running for mayor in a nearby town. He went up to the car to make sure that everything was okay and he knew that everyone was a potential vote for him. I was told that the husband's attitude changed drastically and the situation turned totally around. The husband was now Mr. nice guy.

4

The Flood of 1932

I awakened on a Monday morning to find our home full of neighbors sitting wherever they could find a spot. All of those who were fortunate enough to survive the swift and swirling flood waters had taken to the mountainside during the night, only to return after daylight the next morning and witness the damage that had been done to their homes. Many of their homes no longer existed, washed completely away, while others had been swept from their foundation. We were blessed that our home was a higher elevation than many.

The flood of 1932 was devastating for many of the residents of Paint Creek. Although I was young, certain memories stay with me. I went to bed on Sunday evening at my usual time knowing that I had to get up early the next day for school. It started raining on Sunday afternoon after a very muggy day. The rain continued into the evening and through the night. Not only was there nonstop rain but also there was nonstop lightning throughout the night. Before daylight on Monday morning the damage had been done. Paint Creek had overflowed its banks.

All along Paint Creek, what had once been highly prized household possessions could be seen, intermingled with trash, trees, dead animals and other debris. Many residents up and down Paint Creek lost their lives that fateful night.

Railroad tracks were completely destroyed in many sections, trees were uprooted in the creek bed and sections of bridges were swept away and in some areas the bridges were moved many yards from their foundations. Coal cars were upended, cast along both sides of the stream far from their original settings. Along the country road that wound its way along Paint Creek earth slides had come off the steep mountainside every few feet making it impossible to get from place to place by car. The coalmine tipples in many places were destroyed.

People stayed at our house two nights and one day. They just sat around because there were too many to lie down. My mom started cooking to feed them. It was dark because some of the lights were out, especially the lights on the side of the road where we walked up and down the highway.

One car went into the water, before the bridge washed away. One black lady drowned. Her baby was recovered in a small basket floating on the water. All the others in the car got out. I don't know which one, but someone saved the baby.

People that lived near the creek had to leave home for their own safety. One lady had her newborn baby buried a short distance behind her house and the flood washed the grave away.

An elderly couple, living across the railroad tracks from our home, was never seen again. Dad and I would go to their home on Sunday morning before church to buy fresh eggs, milk and chicken. It was very sad.

A black family owned a small store that washed away in the flood. They had one child, and, lived in the back of the store; they were the Nolans. The daughter's name was Lynn. This family was also not seen after the flood. The flood of 1932 goes down in history as one of the most devastating events on Paint Creek.

5

High School to College

By the time I entered the eleventh grade and was attending high school in Montgomery, which was about 20 miles from Milburn, there were enough children to justify a school bus for our area. Montgomery was the largest and closest town around and it had many stores and even an amusement park. This meant that I could stay at my own house during the week and catch the school bus rather than staying over with relatives or neighbors that were on the bus route. It was during these times that I started to learn how to play the piano at a friend's house and actually enjoyed it. Some Saturdays, my friends and I would catch a transporter bus from Milburn to Montgomery for 75 cents and we would spend the time shopping and just enjoying the sights.

Whatever was going on in any of the communities on Paint Creek the children would talk about it on the school bus, or when they came to the theatre to see the movies. While attending Montgomery High School an assistant school superintendent would come to our school to speak. He would encourage us to stay in school, and do the right thing, and most of all stay out of trouble, but very few were listening. We liked the fact that when he showed up we did not have to go to class. I don't ever remember any of the white members in the school system coming to speak at our school.

It was during this time that I met one of my dearest friends, Whenever there was something going on at school I would stay at the Ruth's house. Her mom and dad were great people. Her dad was a deacon in the church, and her mom was one beautiful lady, and very kind to me. This became my home away from home. Ruth's parents could see us as we walked to school. It was almost the same as grade school at home because it was such a short distance. Ruth's family had the same nourishing type meals that I had become accustomed to at home. The rules at Ruth's house were even similar to those at home. The family lived in town close to school and church. Ruth and I enjoyed each other's company and we had many wonderful times together.

At lunchtime Ruth and I would go downtown to Coney Island. This was an amusement area where there were rides, games and refreshments. It would be in full swing on the weekends. Coney Island had the best and cheapest hot dogs. We would get our hot dogs, and go back to Ruth's house, because she could really make a great cup of coffee. I would tease her, for she would take more time than was allowed, but it was worth waiting for.

I needed an excuse to go downtown, but Ruth didn't because she lived in town and I didn't. I had to have an excuse to pass to the school patrol guy. Excuses were stamped every day so we couldn't use the same one twice. We were not allowed to leave the premises without an excuse for any reason. This particular time, I was caught without an excuse. The patrolman lived in Milburn where I did and he turned my name in along with five others. I wasn't allowed downtown for a week. This was the first, and only incident that took me to the principal's office. The principal was a minister in the community of Montgomery. He was also a businessman, and a genuinely nice guy who did not tolerate foolishness.

I got a reprimand for my disobedience. None of us wanted to hear it but we didn't have any choice. I made myself a promise, not to let this happen again, and it didn't. After that we would write excuses for each other addressed and dated from each hometown and forged a parent signature. Still not quite total obedience.

This same patrolman that reported me to the principal turned my name in for talking about him on the bus, that's why I snatched away his written prayer while he was praying at church during prayer meeting. If a patrolman turned your name in, they would take his word, no exceptions, and no questions asked. The rules were: no bad behavior, no fighting or disturbance of any kind, while on the bus or you would be expelled. That was the one and only time for me, because I had no intentions of being expelled.

We were sitting on the Ruth's porch one day when a twelve-year-old boy jumped in a neighbor car and took off. The neighbor had left their keys in the car. The street was very narrow and downhill. The boy crashed into two cars. Luckily he wasn't hurt and no one was in the parked cars. His parents were liable even though the keys were there. An accident not waiting but did happen. I'm sure he got in trouble for that stunt.

When I was a senior in high school, I had my wisdom tooth pulled. The solution that I was using (Listerine and salt water), I would hold it in my mouth for an extended period of time. Instead of moving the solution around in my mouth I just held it in one position. My dad saw me and he told me I needed to move my mouth about while using the solution, but I didn't at the time because my mouth was so sore and for that reason my jaws locked. I couldn't eat or talk for a week, just sipping liquid through a straw.

One of my friends, and I were studying together. This was our second year taking French and someone stole my brand new French book and we had to study for a test. I had to write my answers on paper.

The senior prom was special. The school gymnasium was lit up like a Christmas tree. We knew what to expect. There were two adults on every entrance, and they seemed to be stationed wherever we ended up. They could see everything going on in the room. The kids weren't really bad; the teachers just didn't want any problems. We all had a wonderful time.

Life in College

Ruth and I graduated from high school and went off to Bluefield State Teachers College. The white college was Bluefield State College and the black college was Bluefield State Teachers College. It was a new environment for me, but the rules didn't change much. When we left the dormitory we had to sign out, and when we returned we signed back in. The staff was nice and things were fairly normal with the exception of two female professors who didn't like each other. I discovered later that it was over a man they both liked.

There was a football game one particular weekend, and Mr. Madden, a professor from another school, was giving his attention to Miss Jacobs, and Miss Brennen got wind of it and did not like it. Everyone thought she was his girlfriend and apparently she thought so as well. When she saw them together she became loud and rude. She forgot, that the dean did not tolerate such nonsense. She wanted to get close enough to the other lady to start trouble. At this point, Mr. Madden got two of his buddies to carry her away from the scene, before she made a spectacle of herself.

We were so surprised at the behavior of Professor Brennen. Mr. Madden didn't want the police involved, because no one wanted a scandal. He stayed with Miss Jacobs through it all and Miss Brennan knew he wasn't with her. She was embarrassed about the incident but tried not to show it. The drama did not stop there; she waited in her car until after the game, and tried to run them over. She hit the car from behind as they were trying to get in. No one was hurt, but everyone on campus knew what was happening. She knew students knew, but she never said I'm sorry.

There was one girl in our group that decided to move out of the dormitory into an apartment. She said she just wanted to be alone, to collect her thoughts. She had enough money to move but didn't have a job. She had a month to have peace and quietness. When the rent was due, and her notice came in the mail she sent the bills to her dad. No one told her to get an apartment. She just wanted to prove to us, that she could do what she wanted on her own. When she picked up her mail a week later, her dad sent the bills that she had acquired back to her, and told her they weren't his, because they weren't in his name. Finally, she accepted what her dad said, get a job. She ended up right back on campus with the rest of us. Sharing a dorm room with a fellow student.

Professor Brennan, the professor with the bad attitude, had a brother name Jack who was married with three children, and wouldn't work in a pie shop. His wife had a job at a restaurant. His wife's name was Sybil. Professor Brennan helped out by buying food and clothes for the children. Her brother Jack appeared to be satisfied doing nothing. She would even go over sometimes to cook and help around her brother's house.

The children were in grade school. She would share with us during class what was going on over at her brother's house. She said he always kept the television, and couch occupied. She was so angry about the situation that she would talk about it and didn't care who heard. She described him as trying to be a big shot. She said he always kept the best of everything for himself, including food. He didn't associate with others because he didn't want to hear what his neighbors had to say. His sister continued to help them, because she didn't want the authorities involved.

Professor Brennan's brother seemed not to care what people said about him. He was an adult that wouldn't take care of his family. His wife continued to stay with him for whatever reason. I heard he never changed. Professor Brennan said she wondered who would take care of him if he got sick. She said she certainly would not because he never did anything for anyone.

One of the students that had an apartment in the city was looking for a roommate. This was the same young lady that had moved out of the dormitory sometime earlier. This time she moved in with April. Mona then got a job at the drugstore. The girls knew each other for a few months. They lived together for about two months. Mona paid the first month's rent. Then she began spending her money foolishly and started being late with her rent. She never realized there's a difference when you're living with someone else. She started buying clothes and jewelry. She had no idea, that it was time to grow up and that there would be no one around to help her all the time. It was the second time around for Mona. She told her roommate, she needed a couple of weeks to get herself together, but the roommate was too angry to reason with her. She just packed all of Mona'a clothes while she was at work, and told her if you don't pick up your things after class, I will throw them out. She didn't pick up her stuff for a couple of days.

Mona had the habit of smoking. We were not allowed to smoke in our rooms, not even in the building, just outside. Some of the girls smoked in their rooms anyway. They just never got caught. My friend Ruth and I were roommates. We never smoked, and we didn't let anyone else smoke in our room. It didn't make sense to have smoking in our room when neither one of us smoked. Mona was always borrowing things like clothes and jewelry. She had a necklace that she wore only in the evening, never to class, because we thought she stole it. We stopped hanging around with her, because she was like an accident, waiting to happen.

A bracelet was taken from the drugstore, where Mona worked, it was costume jewelry and cheap at that. One white girl worked at the same store. The owner blamed Mona. He really didn't see who took it. If she had it, we never saw it in her possession. It was never found. At least that's what was told to us. Mona just did so many strange things. That was the only time I ever saw the police come around the dormitory. They wanted to know if anyone saw this particular bracelet. She was the only black that had access, because the other girl was white. She wasn't caught with the goods. If that had happened, they would have sent her to jail. I am so glad it never came to that. She was eventually fired from her job at the drugstore.

Everyone at school knew Mona was a troublemaker. Her boyfriend was looking for a car. The car dealer let him test-drive a couple of cars. He hadn't decided which one he wanted, so by coincidence they left the keys in one of the cars. He hadn't planned to get either one. He just wanted to ride around, but Mona intercepted the keys, picked up another girl, and went joy riding. She told her friend, that she was considering buying the car. She drove around all evening. She was asking for trouble.

The car dealer had two car lots, and one employee at each one, because business wasn't that great. Mona got a break, and took the car back safely. I never went any place with her, because you can be in the wrong place at the wrong time. She enjoyed the ride so much, that she went back to the car lot and did it again, because she never got caught.

One afternoon the music professor sent word for Mona and me to come to her office. The school had a great singing group, and wanted us to join. We were in another class when we got the news, but I decided not to go at that time—especially with her. When I got to practice there was another girl there that I didn't particularly like, because she thought that she was all that, and then some—maybe she didn't particularly care for me either. Upon second thought, she probably didn't even know me. I never got the opportunity to join the singers. They sang on the radio twice a week. Maybe my decision not to try out for the group wasn't a smart thing to do. Everybody makes mistakes, and that was only one of mine.

We often went to the movies while in college. We didn't go much during the week. Most of us went on Saturday afternoon. It was always around noon and we would go in a group. The blacks had to go around an alley, and go up a flight of stairs. It was not an alley that you could drive through. It was just a dead end street. We had to be in at seven anyway. We never let dark catch us in the alley. Once we were inside we sat in the balcony, all blacks did.

We could buy popcorn, soft drinks, and other snacks, but we were not allowed to sit down on the first floor of the theatre and we didn't have the same entrance or exit.

We were coming out of the theatre one evening and two young white guys passed by in a truck. They were looking for trouble. We never looked at them. They kept saying, "Where are you all from?" As if we were from another planet, and "do I know you?" We kept silent, as we walked. Some weekends there would be one or two guys with us, but that day it was six of us, all girls. At that time, they wanted to know if we wanted a ride. We kept silent. They never got out of the car. I don't think they really wanted to. There was no incident that day but it was an uncomfortable situation.

Shortly after I got to college, two other friends and I began talking among ourselves about the subjects we were taking. I began to think about all the time that I had spent in school, and even though it was a good thing, I felt I was missing out on life. Time is life; it is irreversible, and irreplaceable. Take advantage of both, because everything revolves around time.

There is an old expression that time is money. I believe it to be true. It's important to make the most of the time we have and to spend it wisely. It is good common sense. As you go about your busy day and don't accomplish what you want to do to consider people that are busier, yet accomplish much more than yourself. As for me, I wonder where the time goes.

In this life it's good to have a plan, even though plans are made to be changed. For one thing, it is to our advantage to take the time to set our priorities in order.

6

The Bus Trip

My dad's brother died, and I went to Alabama on the greyhound bus for the funeral. The ride south was pretty uneventful and there was no trouble. Although the occasion was sad, it was good to spend time with family.

While in Alabama, three friends and I were riding around, and we decided to park and chat. All of a sudden, a police car came speeding into the neighborhood. We later learned that there had been a domestic dispute. There were two cops, one white, and one black. I didn't want to believe what I saw. The white cop had a gun, and the black cop had a stick! That's the way it was. The police stayed about ten minutes, and came out. We concluded that they had the situation under control.

Other than the cops, no one in that house came out, which was very unusual. The cops had a brief discussion outside, and moved on. As soon as they were out of sight, they were called back. A lady came running out of the house and behind her was a guy about six feet tall with a knife in his hand. The woman was small in frame and I wondered why the guy would even need a knife. The cops commanded the man to drop the knife. He eventually did comply with the officers' request but he looked at the black cop and said, where is your gun? The police had no choice, but to take him to jail, because he continued to be disrespectful.

I spent four days in Alabama and was on my back home to Paint Creek. The comedy started as soon as I got on the bus. A black couple got on behind me. I was already seated. There was no room for them to sit together. I wondered why the man boarded the bus before the woman. He sat down beside a white lady setting in front of me, so the woman with him sat down beside me. She had the nerve to ask the lady to exchange seats with her, and she refused. They had been drinking, because it smelled something awful.

The man kept running his mouth, but the lady ignored him, and never said a word. The black lady harassed the white lady until we arrived at another station. The crazy conversations continued. A couple of black guys boarded the bus at the next stop. They proceeded by asking a nicely dressed white gentleman: Where did you get that suit? The guy was minding his own business. They kept harassing the man, saying all sorts of ridiculous things. They even called him names.

The passenger being harassed agreed to everything the guys said, he even said he would buy them a drink when the bus made a stop. Most of the passengers had issues, you wouldn't believe. One of the black guys was commenting about the advertisements on the inside of the bus walls. The guy was trying to tear them off the side and the top of the bus, as far as the he could reach. It was during this time that the black man sitting next to the white lady went to the restroom. When he returned, he sat in the lady's lap, as if he didn't know he was not in his seat. She started screaming. He kept falling all over her, as if he couldn't help it. He just wouldn't mind his own business.

Finally, the bus driver who happened to be white, decided to see what the problem was. There were about ten white people including him on the bus. The other passengers were black. He was a real nice guy, and just wanted to keep everything in order, so that he could keep his schedule. Somehow, he was able to reason with the guy causing the disturbance and even though he continued to talk nonstop he was not as loud.

When we got to Louisville, Kentucky, a white lady was parked and apparently waiting for the bus we were on. She pulled up right across the street to pick up one of the passengers on the bus. I got off for about five minutes, but I never left the area. Another car pulled up beside the same car that was parked. The guy that got out of the second car left his door open so no one could pass. He was carrying a gun and it didn't take much to realize that he was looking for trouble. I breathed a sigh of relief to see him move on, before anyone called the police.

It just so happened that I had been carrying a box of pecans on my lap since I boarded the bus in Alabama. I should have mailed those pecans. I had gathered the pecans from my uncle's yard and they were by this time an unnecessary bother and drew more attention to me than I cared for. I sensed that some of the passengers thought that I was carrying something valuable. Eventually, I decided to put the box on the luggage rack and the attention of the passengers left the box and me and I traveled peacefully for the rest of the ride home.

The trip from Alabama was long and tiring and at this particular juncture, the bus driver was near a small town where he had to slow down. I happened to be looking out of the window on the side of the highway. There was a river and on the bank of the river was a man and a lady fishing. Another guy approached the couple walking toward the river and pushed the woman in the water. I suppose he knew her. I'm sure she was surprised at his action. The guy that was with the lady ran after him. We were in traffic, so I didn't see if the other man caught him. I had no idea what was going on. I just observed the incident from my window on the bus. The whole scene got me to laughing and helped to lift my mood.

I always liked daytime traveling on the bus, because you can see the countryside. It was now time to change buses, and I was one hour away from where one of my sisters lived. More passengers got on the bus and about five minutes later, the driver came around to collect the tickets. The bus driver said I'm one ticket short. One black guy didn't have a ticket. I am pretty sure that the bus driver knew this before now. He went to the rear of the bus and since the guy could not produce a ticket he quietly left the bus. I felt sorry for him, and at the same time, it was embarrassing, but I'm sure he knew he couldn't ride free. He probably didn't have any money.

This was the same man in the bus station that had been asking other passengers for money. One lady asked me if he asked me for money. I said no, he asked me what time did the bus leave? He didn't even ask me what destination. I told him I had no idea, to ask the ticket agent. After that I didn't say anything more to him and I wasn't interested in pursuing the conversation.

I was quite happy for this trip to end.

7

Some Things Don't Pay

One day after class, two friends and I were in a department store just browsing and not looking for anything special. One of the clerks, a white lady came over and asked if she could help us. We thanked her, and said we were just looking. All of a sudden she started crying. We could see there was something wrong. She started telling us about her problem. The clerk said, she had always found a way to keep her son away from his dad, for whatever reason. She said she would take him to relatives out of town, and leave him for weeks at a time, before bringing him home, after that, she would leave him with other people. Both families were nearby.

Her son was eight years old. It was now time for her break. She kept saying for years she has been upset with her husband, even though he never mistreated her. She said she had no real reason for this behavior. It just seemed right at the time. As she looked around, as a family member brought her son into the store. He wanted nothing to do with her. Her son had never had a relationship with his dad. His name was Burke. In front of us all he told her how he hated his mom.

Burke is a man now, but he doesn't have anything to do with his mother. She's sick, but nothing has changed, as far as Burke is concerned. He visits his dad as much as possible but he resents the fact that he missed out on his childhood with his dad. His mom apologized to him, but he felt no different. She would call him on his birthday, but he does not take her calls.

Burke's dad never tried to take him from his mother, because he knew that Burke needed both parents. The mother spent all that time keeping her son away from his father and therefore the son missed his dad's point of view on many things in life. In the meantime, those that he was around did not necessarily have his best interest at heart anyway. Time is God's gift to us for the moment or a day at a time. Burke blamed his mother for many of his bad habits because he didn't have the supervision of his father.

I knew a very nice lady named Sybil. We were just walking around one morning when we ran into her cousin who had smoked for years. She told us that the doctor told her to stop smoking and walk everyday. A couple of her friends were holding her up. She could barely stand, and was trying to walk. Can you believe she had a cigarette in her hand? The cigarettes had already destroyed her lungs. Last I heard, she was still smoking, telling us, that the doctor didn't know what he was talking about, and that she never took the medicine anyway. I said to Sybil how would she know whether it worked or not, if she didn't take it. While we were talking, one of the women that were trying to hold Sybil's cousin up lit a cigarette; that was some ordeal; thank God, we were outside.

We left the area, and went to lunch. There was a white couple in line, in front of us. This man pushed the woman he was with down in front of everybody. I couldn't believe what I saw. While she was down, he walked away for a moment. I would say about three minutes. Another couple, also in line picked her up before he returned. The woman got up crying. It was such a sad situation. The man came back and acted as if nothing happened.

After lunch we were leaving the restaurant and ran into the same couple. It seemed that he was really was trying to get away from her. He got in the car, and so did she. He then pushed her out on the pavement. He wasn't trying to help her, but she didn't seem to mind. Someone wanted to call for help but she said no. We could see that she was hurt because she had the scars to prove it. Someone called anyway, because the people at the restaurant thought her injuries may be extensive, and they didn't want any publicity. I found out later that this lady stayed in this abusive situation for years.

There was a black lady in the crowd that knew him, because she worked for his mother at one time. She said he always lived with his parents. They let him stay, and he never worked, because they took care of him. He never realized, that no one else would do this when they were no longer around.

He never married the woman; I found that out by chance. I wasn't interested in the way she was being treated, because in my estimation it was such a sad situation. She had a good job working at a bookstore, and flower shop. I wonder what she was thinking when she let him spend her money, and still didn't get a job. This guy was driving his family's car. Still the abuse continued, fighting her anyplace, anywhere and anytime, just like some of the guys in my hometown, and other parts of Paint Creek. His name always came up in the newspaper. She continued to ride with him.

One day they were in the car together. He was driving too fast as usual. He had been drinking and lost control of the car and ran off the road and hit a tree. The woman was thrown out of the car and over a small embankment. Her friends wondered why she had anything to do with him at all. She lived twenty-four hours unconscious and died. The write up in the paper stated that he showed no remorse. He had a few bruises and was shaken up a bit. After taking him to the hospital, the police took him to jail. The woman's family got a lawyer. With his track record, her family wanted the death penalty. He was given fifteen years. His parents couldn't get him out on bail, because the authorities knew he was a bad risk. In jail, he forgot that he wasn't there on vacation, but to be punished, and to take orders. He had to get beat up a couple times to face reality. He told his buddies that he slipped and fell off a ladder while painting.

No one else came to visit him, because he really didn't have any real close friends. His family was always there. Other than his father and mother, people never respected him. He was just another number like everyone else there.

One lady that worked at the prison, met him, and began being nice to him; even though she found out he was there for murder. It made no difference to her, he began telling her about his prison experience, and how the guys would say and do things to get him in trouble. He had no help, and she felt sorry for him.

She began to do things for him, such as buying cigarettes, snacks, soft drinks, and books to read. He tried to do better, but it wasn't really in him to be nice. At first he didn't even know how to say thanks for her good deeds.

A friend of mine had a cousin in the same jail. All that wasn't in the papers, he would tell her. Keith was what you would call one of a kind. When he met Terry, he figured this was his second chance to do well. When she began trying to help and get him out of prison, she said he was doing better. After five years, he didn't do anything to cause real trouble so they promised to let him out on parole, if he had a job. He made her a promise that after he was out he would marry her. When they let him out Terry let him come to live with her. She got him a job at the grocery store. He worked there for a year, and did very well, even though he never had the word responsibility in his vocabulary. She worked nights at an all night diner. He worked days, and on weekends, he would have card parties, and sell drinks, especially when she wasn't home.

One night she came home early, and was very upset to find a noisy crowd. She told him to get everybody out immediately because he could not afford a police call. She said he didn't want a return trip to prison for any reason, and certainly not for selling alcohol illegally, and disturbing the peace. She decided to leave this headache behind, so they went their separate ways.

Keith was like the husband of an old friend of mine, that I grew up with. She was a great lady, and she told me how nice he was. This guy wanted to get married right away, but she decided to wait a few months to get to know him.

He was nice for about six months. Both of them had jobs. She began to tell me how he was acting. First of all he would help pay the bills, but didn't want her to have any money. He knew she wasn't well, but didn't try to help her in any way. In fact he would talk about her being sick all the time as if she could help it. He wasn't well himself, but he wasn't as sick as she was. She said he never asked, "How are you?" Or "can I help you in any way?" He would say negative things like, "there is nothing wrong with you," or "stop complaining, you can do more than you do." She said other than gas she wasn't supposed to have any money.

She had her own home, and he moved in with her. In other words he was trying to control her. She wouldn't let him, and that he didn't like. She really wanted this to work because her men friends always wanted to take advantage of her, because she was nice. For one thing, he didn't want her to have any friends; he would always insult them, and take her out to eat and act silly as if he couldn't afford whatever she wanted to eat. She decided to get rid of him once and for all. She ordered a couple of dinners, and extra stuff for other people there. She went to the restroom, and never came back. She got a ride and went home. He was left with the bill. It was more money than he was holding. For once he was embarrassed. The owner didn't call the police, because he had some of the money. They made him do the dishes, and clean up the place.

This incident gave one of the waitresses a wake up call. She had been going to work everyday. Her husband was home in bed enjoying the good life while she was out working. One morning when she got to work, she turned around, went back home, and jumped on him. This was to let him know how ridiculous it was to lie around while she did all the work.

I know of another guy that wouldn't work, that lived in another small town near Paint Creek. His name was Mandy. He was a white guy, but was friends with a black guy. They were almost inseparable and when you saw one, you would see the other. The black guy's name was "Gus". Neither one kept a job. They were accused of breaking into a warehouse. They knew a guy that worked there. It was no problem to get in, so they thought. The guy that was supposed to let them in was detained, and never made it in time. It made absolutely no difference to them they broke in anyway and took radios, clocks, small tables, kitchen stools. They had a car, not a truck, so their space was limited and they could only carry so much. They didn't get caught at that time. There was no one around, but they did know, that crime doesn't pay, and you don't take what doesn't belong to you. The guy that was supposed to leave the door open was wise, in not showing up. The guys wanted to try again. The employee said he would not open the door. He had come to his senses and had decided that he didn't want to go to jail.

Two cousins went hunting. Each one had a son; one was ten and the other was twelve. They took them hunting, but it was suppose to be a camping trip. Somehow, the kids were playing around, when their dads weren't looking. The gun discharged, and hit one of the boys in the arm. They had to bring him out of the woods. They drove to the closest hospital, which was seventeen miles away. The doctor's office had closed for the day. Sometimes he would leave early, and his house was five or six miles away. There was no telephone close by. They were fortunate because it was a flesh wound. They didn't know this until they arrived at the hospital, because of all the blood. The boy got better. They kept him in the hospital for a couple of days. Even though they called this a freak accident. They didn't learn very much from the accident because they still kept guns around the house.

The boy's mother was arguing with his dad about the accident. She grabbed one of the guns, and pointed it at him, because they were saying that, they weren't supposed to be loaded. The sheriff heard about all the news, and about the accident and went to their house to check out the story. In those days the sheriff did not bother anyone about a gun, unless they shot somebody and the ones that had guns didn't have to get them registered.

8

The Beautician and Others

There was very little work for the women on Paint Creek unless you got a job in the company store, the post office, or doctor's office. These jobs were usually given to select people and vacancies were far and few. If a woman was a teacher, or you had a special skill like hair styling, sowing, cooking, etc. she had an advantage over those that did not have these abilities or training.

Gwen moved to Paint Creek from Chester, Pennsylvania and ran a small beauty shop out of her home. During this time, they were referred to as beauticians. Today we would call them hair stylists. Gwen worked in a gun shop in Charleston during the week and on the weekend she would do hair. There were few business for women on Paint Creek.

Gwen's shop was open Friday afternoon and all day Saturday. There was no competition because her shop was the only one for miles around and she did well. Gwen had a very nice husband. He was hard working and went to church regularly. I never heard anything negative about this guy. He would speak and mind his own business. His name was Gerald. He worked in the coalmines and had a side business. One weekend Gwen came home with a young couple that she had recently met and offered them room and board in exchange for household chores and help to her husband. Her husband Gerald had customers that would buy wood from him to keep from having to chop it.

Gerald worked with a white guy with a truck. The two of them would cut trees down, and chop them up to fit fireplaces and wood and coal stoves. They would stack the wood inside and on the porch. Gerald also had a small woodshed outside to store the extra wood. Joe started out good as a helper but got greedy. He started keeping part of the money he received from sales instead of selling the wood by the load. He discovered he could make more by selling small bundles; such as, a dozen sticks for a dollar and a half.

Gwen came home one weekend and heard about what Joe had been doing. She did not wait for her husband to so that they could confront Joe as a couple. There was an argument, and shortly thereafter the neighbors saw Joe running from Gwen and Gerald's home. The passenger bus just happened to be passing and Joe stopped the bus, and jumped on. He didn't take time to get his clothes. He even left his wife. Some say it was good, that he left, because it would have been a bad scene. Gwen told the neighbors what was going on even though most knew anyway. Joe was never seen again in the neighborhood.

Gwen had tried to help the couple. Joe didn't have a job when she met him and she resented the fact that he was trying to cheat her. Judy left the next day because she did not want to stay without Joe.

Gwen had a habit of yelling and talking loud to her husband whenever they were together. Anyone that knew them knew about this. She would embarrass him wherever they were: church, home, outside the home, anywhere at anytime. She was loud, and he was just the opposite. Gwen made friends that she couldn't keep, because of a bad attitude. Eventually, Gwen and Gerald moved away and the neighbors were happy to see her leave though they did miss the beauty shop.

In all the communities, most people knew other people's business because there was always someone around to tell it. It was almost a type of entertainment; black or white, there was always a news flash. All you had to do was to go to the local company store. There was a white family of about eight people that lived on Paint Creek. They lived in a large house, compared to the four rooms most people lived in. Twin brothers lived there that worked in the coalmines. One of the brothers was married to the lady of the house. She would do the shopping. Take care of the children and the home and was known to sit on the porch everyday and smoke a cigarette or two. Her name was Amelia and most people knew her.

Amelia's husband got sick and about a year later, he died. They continued to live in the large house. Amelia shocked the community by marrying her husband's brother. The brother continued to work in the coalmines, just as he did when his brother was alive. Of course people talked because they had nothing better to do. The couple seemed to ignore the talk and continued their lives in the community as they always had until the brother was laid off his job and the family moved.

When the miners wanted something done they would strike. As the working hours decreased and the coalmines began working half the time, some even two and three days a week, many families decided to leave Paint Creek. Work was so bad, that many white families left the community, and the coalmine management began to allow black families to move into the larger houses. One black couple that moved into the community, the wife's name was Sylvia, started selling refreshments such as cigarettes, candy, sodas, and anything she felt was good to eat. She didn't have a license, but no one cared at that time. She only sold her goods when the general store, and poolroom was closed. That meant weekends and after noon on Saturday.

One Saturday evening, three white teenagers came for candy, and most of all cigarettes, they lied about their age. One of them lit a cigarette in her house, and started a fire. Sylvia came back before it got out of hand. They threw water around just in time. After the clean up Sylvia kept her little business going, but she got rid of the cigarettes, which shouldn't have been there in the first place.

About a week later, there was a fight. Again, the teenagers didn't respect Sylvia's home, too many congregated there listening to the radio, and dancing. They started throwing things, and really messing up the house. After this incident, Sylvia gave up the idea of having a snack bar.

Some of Sylvia's family members were jealous of her success in having extra money and being able to acquire more things than they possessed. A family feud started. One day some children were fighting her daughter and none of her cousins, who happened to be present, came to her rescue. Sylvia's daughter was hurt pretty bad in the dispute. This was a wake up call for the whole family. Finally, the pastor of the local church called them together, to try and help. This was a family acting like strangers and fighting among themselves. The family began to see how senseless it was to keep up such behavior and the situation turned for the better.

Wherever I went, I looked forward to coming back home to Paint Creek. I always made it home for holidays. My mom and dad bought the biggest turkey they could find and we would have a wonderful time as a family. My dad didn't go shopping with the family very often, maybe once a year. He told my mom that she backtracked too often while shopping.

We were shopping once when I saw a black man get kicked out of a white bar. We laughed and made light of it because everyone knew that there were some places blacks did not even consider going. A white bar was definitely one of those places.

There was a teenage couple that lived in one of the local towns. You might say Nathan, was quite a bit older, but Sheena was his girlfriend. They had been friends for some time. I went to school with Nathan, a very nice guy. He was my boyfriend in high school, and one day Sheena was found dead on the bank near running water where people fished. No one knew for sure what happened, people fished in this location often, white and black, but Nathan was the first suspect. Sheena had a boyfriend and an ex-boyfriend. I don't believe Nathan did it. Both guys went to jail for her murder. I forget how long they stayed. They never found out what happened, and Nathan died early in life. I don't think he was even middle age.

9

Love and Life

One day a group of us young people were coming from Montgomery on the passenger bus when I met William. William was a handsome young man but what I noticed more than anything else was that William was never at a loss for words. He would have something to say about everything. My first reaction to him was not favorable. I later ran into William at the theater and shortly thereafter we started seeing each other on a regular basis. He soon started saying to his friends and anyone who would listen that he was going to marry me. One day William caught my dad coming from work and asked him if he could marry me. When I asked him, what did my dad say? He said, I don't know, I didn't wait to see. He asked him and ran away without waiting for an answer.

About a year later, William and I got married at the courthouse along with a couple of friends for witnesses. It took me all day to show my dad the marriage certificate. Dad surprised me and said if you had waited, I would have given you a wedding. We had a nice reception anyway and I was satisfied with that. A small wedding would have been nice, but the courthouse was good enough for me.

Our first child died at birth and our second child died of pneumonia at the age of five months. Both experiences were quite painful. I was to eventually have four more sons and two daughters. When my fifth child was born, I was paralyzed from the waist down for about six weeks. The doctors found no reason for the paralysis. I went home. No one suggested therapy. They ran all kinds of tests and nothing seemed to help. My good friend Bell Turner and her husband Jim always helped me with the children. She would lift me out of bed. I was weighing about 110 pounds. I did all I could to work with my own legs to get back to normal.

One Sunday I went to a revival meeting in a wheel chair, and a white minister prayed for me. I began to get better, and have use of my legs, doing whatever movement I could, as my mom and others would massage my legs. I made it through that ordeal, and had three other children. The all black school they attended wasn't very far. By the time my children were ready for school a new school had been built. I only had two old enough to go. I always had them walk with the children next door. They were older children.

One night my husband came home after working the afternoon shift. It was about eleven thirty. After a shower and snack I heard him in the back room, we had a four room house. He was praying out loud. I opened the door and said: "you're going to wake up the neighbors if you don't stop that noise." He didn't stop until he was ready. He did this for about a half an hour, and then he went to sleep. The baby slept through the night but I got sick and didn't get a chance to rest at all. It was one of the most miserable nights of my life. I had no right to disturb him, as he was giving praise and thanks to God. From that day on, I never tried to hinder him again. I grew up in church, and prayer and praise had always been a part of my life. I learned a lesson in this. If you don't want to do the right thing, it's not a good idea to hinder someone else. You will reap what you sow, whether good or bad.

When my last child was born, I was in the hospital for two weeks, because of complications. My husband came to pick me up on a Monday. I had been home a week from Monday when he went to work, and was killed in a coal mining accident. My baby was three weeks old. This was a devastating time in my life.

It was about 8:00 p.m. in the evening when my dad and a good friend and neighbor Elder Bohanna knocked on my door. What are you doing here I said to them? Then Elder Bohanna said: "your husband just got killed." My dad immediately began to comfort me. He always knew what to say. We relied on him for that. It was difficult to hear those words and for a while I could not process them.

I was told that the miners had been using dynamite to remove the coal that they were loading inside the mines. William went further back into the mines for a load of the coal on his buggy and the top of the mines collapsed around him and he was covered with coal and dust from the coal. An ambulance was called as soon as it happened, and it probably took about 40 minutes before the ambulance arrived. By the time they removed him from the coal dust and drove the nineteen miles to the nearest hospital, he had passed. I was a widow at an early age with six children. The oldest one was eight years old. (Two had died as minors—one died at birth and the other at five months old with pneumonia)

I relied on my faith in God and the loving support of family and friends. Sometimes I wonder how I got through this ordeal. It was a tough time for me. I tried not to cry unless I was alone. One might as well forget feeling sorry for you because that won't help.

This was an experience you don't want to have, but you learn to live with it, as time goes by. It's kind of like a dream. Life is one way and in a moment it all changes. Most of all you never forget it. And, it is not something that you want to forget because it represents a portion of your life.

My family and my church were all there for me every step of the way. When all the arrangements had been made and the home going service at church was over, I could hardly believe that it had all taken place.

After the death of my husband, some of the ladies in the different communities began to send me messages saying they would take one of the boys to help me out. I sent the message back that there were six, so they would have to take all six to get the one they wanted.

My mom and dad were living and I had two sisters close by, so I had plenty help with the children. My brother in law, Alburn was there to help teach them from a man's point of view. As a mother, I could only teach them from a woman's view.

The mining companies did not have a lot of compassion for the widows of the deceased miners. Widows were expected to move out of the company houses after their husbands passed. To their credit thou, they did provide good benefits for the widows and the children. Thank the Lord I was able to move soon after the accident.

I stayed in Milburn about two weeks after my husband's death and moved about fifteen miles away. I bought a house in Cedar Town a new community of primarily black residents. The house was located about a mile and a half from town. For about a year my children were still in an all black school, and everything was convenient. It was here that my children had their first dog, Scrappy, who later died of what I believed was food poisoning but I do not have proof of it. He was a good dog and the children loved him and he would follow them wherever they went. Our next dog was Peanut who was protective of the house and no one came on our property unannounced.

As the children were growing up, I would babysit for people. At that time, some were unable to pay me. I knew that in the beginning. All my children were in school. I kept other children as a favor to my neighbors. When they got a few coins more than normal they would stop speaking. Some would go another way to avoid seeing me. What they didn't realize was that they were the ones that needed help. Not too many people watch your kids for free. The children didn't want to go home when their parents came for them. I treated the children like they were my own.

The company doctor would come through the community and stop as he saw the children who were under his care. He was carrying everything in his car to give the children shots. This was new to me, because we got shots at the Dr's office and school, but at least they had medical attention, and he kept a record. Each mother would get in line, and call their children. This was a good thing, because I didn't have to get them dressed and ready, it worked for me.

My oldest son William Jr. had to have his tonsils out. I had my insurance card from the coal miners, and my new health card. They admitted him to the hospital, but they would not give him the surgery. I had to return home for the money; which was nineteen miles away. I went back the next day with a check. The hospital didn't want to accept a check only cash. They figured I did not have the price of the surgery. It would have only taken a phone call to verify my insurance. The guy in charge would not make the effort to verify it. I ended up paying cash for my son's surgery. When I sent my receipt from the hospital to the insurance company they mailed my money back to me.

One of my son's teachers really upset me. She would regularly come by my house to eat, because she lived alone, and did not like to cook. She always talked about how nice and cute one of my sons was. He was in the second grade. I knew he always did his homework but when he received his last report card I found that she had failed him and he would have to repeat the grade. After this incident she stopped coming by the house. I eventually got a chance to talk to her on the phone. Her reason for not passing him was if she had passed him, he wouldn't be in her class.

I never saw her again after that, I'm so glad I didn't. I had so many of his school papers and report cards showing good grades. I was thinking about reporting her to the board of education, but she left town for good.

10

A New Friend

I met a young woman at a church I was visiting. The friend's name was Marina and she had a story unlike any that I had heard. Marina was never treated as a family member. Her family did not believe anything she said or did. She was blamed for everything that happened at home. Marina was not trusted or given any responsibilities in her home.

Marina was never given an opportunity to go to the store to purchase a small item, or pay a bill like most teenagers. It was as if she was not part of the family unit. This happened from childhood to adult. Her mother wouldn't even trust her in the simplest matters. I can't imagine how it must have felt, to always be ignored as if you don't exist. She was even punished for things she never did.

Other members of the family would do things, but she was blamed for them. If her brother or sister did something, she would be blamed, and she was the one that was punished.

When Marina was a teenager, one of the boys she knew was a gang leader. His name was Henry, a teenager around eighteen. Henry stayed in trouble. He would steal things which had no value. One day he stole toothpicks and hadn't had anything to eat. He was a weird guy. He beat his girl friend to death and cut her body up and buried her around the community, even in some of the neighbor's yards. Somehow, the police found out he did it. He's still in jail along with a buddy of his whose name is Rowland.

One day Marina got sick, and was taken to the hospital. She was having female problems. They put her in with the grown-ups because she looked older than she really was. When the doctor came by and found out what was happening, he made them put her in the children's ward. Marina was not allowed to divide snacks to the other children in the family even when she was of age to do so. Marina never asked for anything. She just wanted to belong. When she became an adult it didn't get any better. Her family did not treated her like her other siblings. Marina always had to work.

After Marina grew up and married, she asked her family to babysit and they refused. Her sister was jealous of her, because Marina married before she did and her sister was the one that like to talk to the boys. It was always her sister, but as usual, as teenagers, when they didn't make it home on time, guess who, was to blame. Marina and her sister would leave home for a relative's house and end up in the middle of the boys and girls hangout. Her sister would be the leader in going to places other than where they were supposed to be going, but she never got in trouble.

One guy in the crowd was a policeman. No one knew him personally. He was new in town, and hanging out with the youngsters. He knew the boys were putting alcohol in their drinks. One guy drove by and recognized him. He said that the crowd ran him away. The guys were sixteen to twenty years of age. The policeman's name was Pete. They ran him away, but were afraid to beat him up, because policemen usually have a back up.

Marina and Nina went to the store. Nina was carrying eggs when a young man bumped into her and broke the eggs, and they were all over him. She told what had happened, but the usual thing happened, Marina got a whipping for fighting. Marina's cousin Roxy took five one-dollar bills from the church and said it was she. She took the money from the church secretary. Again, the blame was pointed at Marina.

Roxy had a sister that was always going into someone's purse. Whatever went down wherever she was she managed to make it Marina's fault. One time a friend of Roxy's put a carpet tack in the seat at church. She got a whipping for that, because she was there. Two of her friends didn't change their clothes from church. The kids were playing ball, fell down in the dirt and got their very nice clothes dirty.

One day Marina got mad, and had the family dog to bite Roxy. She was tired of getting beaten for something someone else did. Roxy's boyfriend went to the store. His name was Dan and Kelly was with him. Dan stole candy and gifts; they both did it to show off for the girls. They were caught. A lady followed them around. They thought she was shopping. She was working for the store. The guys went outside with the goods, and got caught. They're still doing time for being smart.

Marina's all grown up, has a nice husband, a great family of her own and a good life. Sometimes she says she laughs about her childhood and family life but doesn't hold anything against anyone. She just wants to get the most out of her life from this point on.

11

Change and Challenge

By 1955 I had two daughters and had to take them both to the doctor. They had been going to this doctor about a year. I asked the receptionist for a copy of services rendered. This would be nurse, with no credentials, no identity, and no degree, who came out in a white uniform into the waiting room, all loud before everybody saying "you're not going to get anything." I mentioned the insurance would reimburse me right away.

I had my baby on my lap, and my friend was holding my other daughter, they were ages one and two. The waiting room was full of patients. About four black and eight white patients. Thank God I was holding the baby that gave me a moment to think. I would have been in big trouble, because I would have been all over her, and with six children, I didn't need to be in jail. She was on her job, though I never saw her do anything. I know they would have called the police. Somehow, I had to sit there and take it. The children were sick, and I was where I needed to be. The doctor was really nice. The nurse just wanted to be in control. I know the doctor never knew about this incident.

Since this nurse never handled any medicine, I kept this doctor for a while. One of the younger boys had an allergy. I took him one evening to the same doctor, because she wasn't there in the evening. I was the first one to sign the register. I made the mistake of putting my address down. They knew the neighborhood was black. About two patients went in before me. I went up and told the receptionist, that I was there first. She was real nice and called me next.

It was summer time, and I had plenty of time to get home before dark. I only lived a mile and a half from town. I didn't drive at the time, because I never bothered to learn until later. She called me a cab. It was right around the corner. It was there by the time we came down all those steps.

As we went through town, I saw someone kick a black man out of a white bar. I don't know why he was there in the first place anyway. They were always throwing blacks out of white only bars. I only saw the guy's shoes when he kicked him. It happened before, but it probably wasn't the same guy.

Again, I had to take my baby to the doctor. I called first to see if the one, I didn't want to be bothered with was there. She was not there.

The doctor gave me medicine for her condition and told me what to do. Later that evening, I could see that she wasn't any better. She wasn't a spoiled baby but I had been walking around with her on my hip all evening. When I would try to lay her down. She was holding on for dear life. I didn't go near the stove with her and take a chance on her getting burned. I had to check the food. So I laid her down for a minute. I soon returned to pick her up and she had the strangest look on her face. My neighbor was so close and I asked her to phone the doctor and let him know that I was taking her to the hospital. I was so upset, I couldn't think of his number and I didn't have time to check for his number. When I looked around, a few minutes later, I thought it was my neighbor, coming to take me to the hospital. I couldn't believe my eyes, it was the doctor coming through the front door of my house. He had never been to my house before. He went over to the baby and started working on her. He immediately called for an ambulance.

I knew she was dying when they took her out, even though I had never seen anyone die before. My sister-in-law was next door visiting our in-laws. She told me later that the doctor told her she was going to die anyway. If he thought that, I wonder why he didn't have me take her to the hospital from his office. She didn't tell me at that time because she knew I had too much to deal with. Thank God she didn't tell me until later. No one asked the doctor to come to the house. I just wanted him to meet us at the hospital. It was about five to eight minutes from his office. Linda died that same evening. I had graveside services for her a few days later. This was sixteen months after burying her father. She was my youngest daughter. I had even taken her to the doctor's office earlier that same day. This is why I never finished writing this story. It's not easy remembering it over and over again.

The Telephone and New Neighbors

One of the first things I did when I moved away from Milburn was to go to the telephone company to get a phone. They took the money, but I didn't get a phone for two months. This was almost a totally black neighborhood, but there were about three white families. There were only three black families that had a phone. My oldest sister lived in Pittsburgh. She was very sick, and was trying to call me. When she couldn't get in touch with me, she called the state police. I was a block from them. They called one of my neighbors that lived across the street from me. She had asthma, but she would walk in the snow to get me so I could take the call. That was so ridiculous. The next day I went back to the telephone office. There were phones all around the wall, but they would not give me a telephone.

The following day I wrote a letter to the main office in Charleston. I never thought of consulting with anyone, so that was the first thing that came to mind. It took a couple of weeks, but the local manager came to my house. I didn't know who he was. He was very nice, introduced himself and said I heard you got in touch with the Charleston office. I said yes.

I told him this was an emergency. I have six small children, and I needed a telephone in a new neighborhood. The following week, one of the employees came to the door with an old rusty phone they had taken out of someone else's house. It was all beat up, so I wouldn't let him install it. He said it would be a while. I finally got a phone about a week later. My in-laws and other people also began to get telephones during this time.

In the neighborhood where I lived, there was a small grocery store owned by a black man. He sold mostly dry goods, snacks, cheese and lunchmeat. He had what the customers wanted; cigarettes and low percent alcohol. I happened to stop by for bread and found out he had milk. On the window outside of his store he had a large cardboard sign with red letters. On the sign were names of people who owed him, and how much they owed.

One man walked into the store that had an outstanding bill. A couple of people were laughing. This guy owed him, but he couldn't read anyway so it really didn't make him any difference. On the bottom of the sign were the following words: "owe no man." The ones that owed him didn't care about the sign. Some paid, and some didn't pay anyway.

This was a very interesting time in my life. I was dealing with raising my children as a single mother and I was also very involved in the church and periodically had the opportunity to go out of town for a church council meeting. On one such trip to Tennessee, I remember being on a bus with a friend and we stopped at a certain locations to get something to eat and take a restroom break. At this particular stop we went to the restroom and came back and were really impressed with how nice and large the facility was. We made the same stop on the return trip and returned to the same restroom only to discover that there was a sign that we had missed the first time that said, "whites only." The restroom for blacks was quite small and nothing like the one for whites. We often had similar discrepancies with eating places, which we as blacks had to frequent. Many times I refused to eat on the road because of the attitude of those that served and the cleanliness of the facility.

I was still adjusting to the loss in my life. I didn't know what to do. I thought if I moved away from where it all happened, that it would go away, but it didn't.

12

The Move

Eight years later, I moved to Canton, Ohio. One of my good friends said, you're leaving your home to go and pay rent? I thought I would stay there for a while and all the bad memories would disappear. I hadn't planned to stay in Canton. I just needed a change. In the back of my mind I always thought I would go back to West Virginia. I always wanted to, I just never made an effort to do so. I talked about it, but I never put it into motion.

I realize looking back that the passing of a spouse is different from any other death. I was young, not realizing all the decisions I made were final, no one else to consult. I realized that I should not have left my only sister. I should have stayed in West Virginia and had all those years with her. That will always be with me.

When you don't know what to do at certain times in life take your time and think about what to do. The things that happen to you will not go away and they will always be there. We must deal with them in time.

After I left West Virginia I would set around at night alone thinking about all the sad things that had happened to me, but I could not do anything about it. I was in a new community and I didn't know anyone but my in-laws. It is really something you can't explain; you just live with it the rest of your life.

I didn't know a thing about Canton, even though I had been there before. I had a friend that lived in Canton and I was looking for cheap rent, because this was like a vacation for me. The apartments that were recommended to me were the "projects" (another word for government housing). Before this, I had never heard of projects. They didn't exist where I lived. We always lived in a house. At that time the projects were not a bad place to live. Besides, I don't think it's the projects, as much as the respect one has for others and the way you treat people wherever you are. There are areas that are bad or even worse. I met some great friends in the projects. I never had any problems. Sometimes people just need a chance.

I'm reminded of a lady called Wanda. I knew Wanda talked to my niece, who was a beautician in Montgomery. She resented the fact that the children and I were provided for. She didn't know that Lorie and I were family. Wanda asked her how could I afford to stay home and not work. I'm so glad she didn't ask me. Her husband left her with five children, and she had to work with no added income. I said maybe he didn't work in his lifetime, which made all the difference. Wanda told my niece that where she lived wasn't so great, but I'm sure she was doing the best she could.

When I first arrived in Canton, Ohio; City of the Football Hall of Fame, I began to wonder if this was what I wanted, and whether this move would help me. I eventually did get married for the second time to a kind-hearted quiet man that I had known for sometime. I also moved to Delaware which was about twenty miles from Canton and started attending a church in Delaware. I was attending church one Sunday morning and decided to go up front for prayer because I was going for a physical on Thursday. There were others also in line as we knelt down to pray.

Minister Strain started praying for me and as he was praying, something turned in my left breast, like you would turn a key in a lock. I never thought much about it until the following Tuesday when something fell out of my breast (it was sticking me). I looked down, and began to wonder what is that, and how did it get there? I took it out of my clothing and started thinking what is this? I had no idea what had happened. This was a blessing for me. The Lord had removed this awful thing from my body. It would have caused me a lot of pain and suffering. This was the Lord's doing and it was marvelous in my sight! I began to thank the Lord and give Him praise for bringing me through all the things that had happened to me. The decisions that I had to make down through the years affected my whole family.

I lived in Delaware for several years. Delaware is a great college town. Students come from far and near to go to school. Oh yeah, and once a year, there is the "Little Brown Jug" horse race, and the town is really crowded, because it's the big event of the year.

Eventually I decided that I needed to be close to my children who were now grown so I moved back to Canton. When I visit Delaware now I stay with friends. I'm not there everyday, it's just whenever I'm in town, which is usually once a year. I don't need a hotel.

James and I were together for quite some time before he got sick. He had no chronic illness, he died of old age. He was in the hospital about four weeks and when he died I was there. The nurse asked me if she could get something for me and I said no. I just sat there because I was in shock. I had just talked to him. One of the hospital aides asked me the same thing. The nurse then asked if she should call someone. My answer was the same. The Chaplin came by and prayed with me.

I left the hospital and didn't tell my family until later. I didn't want them to come over. One of my friends was suppose to come over. She never made it. I took my second husband James back to Delaware, Ohio for burial because his family was in the Columbus and Delaware area. After the funeral, one of my grandsons brought me home. I decided to be alone. My children didn't even know that I was back in town. I didn't make any calls, or answer the phone. It's quite a difficult situation, but other than the Lord, you're eventually alone anyway.

13

New Beginning

I was visiting a town nearby with some friends of mine. We were there to see a friend that was having surgery. As we got in the car, I had one foot in the car and one foot on the ground when the driver pulled off. His wife and I were yelling. I was thrown out of the car. When I hit the ground, I started crawling out of the way of the car. He didn't realize what was happening. I knew he had to back up, because he was pulling out into traffic.

It was an accident, I have known both of them since childhood and he never would have done such a thing on purpose. I got up and we continued to the hospital to see my friend.

At the end of the day, I began to feel awful. They wanted to take me to the hospital in the beginning but I refused to go. Eventually, I had to go. They took me to the emergency room and stayed to see that I was okay and brought me back. We spent two hours waiting for the doctor. The nurse was in and out checking on me. Across the hall was a white guy that had been there about half an hour when I saw the nurse direct the doctor to him. I responded by letting the nurse know that I had been waiting for quite a while and she said that I would be next. I had learned a long time ago that you must speak up.

My knees were scarred, but no one touched them. I was given a tetanus shot, and two prescriptions. The next day I came home. A couple of days later I had to go to my regular doctor. His first question was "did they give you an x-ray?" I said "no". He shook his head and sent me for x-rays. I was doing very well, even though my right knee was injured. One doctor recommended surgery but it never happened, and I was fine.

The Locals

When you are a single woman living alone, people often share with you intimate details of their lives. One lady in particular had a husband that drank so much that he would often come home and break up the dishes. The situation got so bad that one day he asked for something to eat and she proceeded to prepare his food, and when she was done she sat the frying pan on the table in front of him to eat out of. He was amazed that he had destroyed every plate that they owned. It was quite a lesson for him.

Like so many others, he let the alcohol control him. He was so abusive that his wife ran away from home every other weekend. It was a sad situation. He was nice to everybody but her. He would take his wife to work. She worked in a diner. He would go to the diner so often, the manager found out who he was. He wouldn't keep a job himself, and wouldn't let her work in peace. She never told her boss who he was but they knew he wasn't there to eat three and four times a day. She was a good worker so they let her keep her job, if he promised to stay away. The customers knew what he was doing, and it wasn't good for business, so he was told not to come back. His name was Patrick, and her name was Jess.

Mr. and Mrs. Preston lived in a nearby town. Mr. Preston went to the office everyday but didn't allow his wife out of the house without him. They didn't have children and it was said that he would beat her often. A friend of mine had a daughter that worked for them. He would tell people she fell down. She wasn't allowed to work, visit friends or have any type of life without him. One day she ran away from her husband while he was at work. He didn't locate her for a couple of months. She got a job, and bought a gun. When he finally found her he began trailing her to find out where she lived. He then broke into her apartment, and attacked her. As he tried to push her down, he got his foot tangled in a cord and fell. That gave her a chance to get away from him. By the time he got up, and reached for her she shot and killed him. She didn't go to jail, because she had a witness that knew he was abusive.

I had company one day and a couple of female friends of mine were saying how they left home so that they could be on their own. They even married older men trying to prove a point. We laughed about it.

One got another boss, and the other one said she got another dad that she could do without.

The Hortens owned several apartments that they would rent and someone was always moving in and out. Mr. Horton knew Patrick and his wife Jess. He and Mrs. Horton decided to give them an opportunity to work for them in exchange for room and board. Things started out okay and soon began to change for the worse.

Patrick started an argument with the boss. Jess couldn't work there. Her family collected enough money for her to get away from him and Jess went to live with another family member trying to get her life in order. The last time I heard anything from him, he was doing the same thing, nothing, and he hasn't found her. I suppose now she can make her own choices. She never had a chance to select anything she wore, or furniture, or anything else concerning everyday living. She said, at one time she wanted a certain chair, and he bought another. She had no say in anything concerning their married life. One black guy I knew had a junkyard. He gave Patrick a job on the recommendation of a good friend. Patrick was later caught carrying things away to sell. As he endeavored to sell the merchandise word got around that he was doing this.

The guy who hired him knew his family and just let him go. He just didn't want the hassle. On his way home he stole two small dogs that were tied to a fence. These dogs belonged to a white couple. They were caring for approximately ten dogs. The two at the fence were small. It was almost dark and he had the nerve to take the dogs and sell them. No one who knew him saw him with the dogs so they never connected him with the theft. Since he got away with that, he became greedy. He went back to the same house and climbed up on the second porch where there was a light. One of the dogs was there and started barking. He backed into some flowerpots, and knocked them over. The neighbors heard the noise, and called the police. When the police arrive, the homeowners answered the door.

They were saying the dogs usually barked for no reason, but the intruder made a lot of noise. He was taken to jail where he spent time for breaking and entering. When he finally got out of jail, he started conducting himself with more decency. His sister told me he still doesn't keep a job, and he drifts from one place to another looking for something free.

That ordeal brought back memories. When I was going to high school there was a family living under a huge rock. We knew that to be a fact, because there was always somebody there. The rock was not far from the roadside. In West Virginia this meant it was on the side of a mountain. This was the area where we would go to pick berries. We laughed, because we didn't know any better. It was a white family. When people passed by them they could care less, they had no other place to go. Otherwise they wouldn't be living under a rock. They were there as long as I could remember. Anytime we passed by, they were always there. You could see clothes lying around on the rocks. As I grew older I realized it wasn't a laughing matter. People do what they have to do. They couldn't do any better and it was no longer a laughing matter. I never heard of anyone trying to help them.

Speaking of help reminded me when my sister was at the hospital having her regular physical. A guy came in sick, and when they found out he had no insurance, he received no further attention other than a Tylenol for his pain. They wouldn't even give him breakfast. This was really sad, but it happens.

The police were looking for a sixteen-year-old relative of mine, because the alleged robber had the first and last name of my relative. The guy the police was looking for was thirty-six. He had stolen something from an old dilapidated service station that most people saw as worthless.

About a dozen policemen, sheriffs and other officers came to my house. I told them that my nephew was in the hospital and had been for two weeks. I said there's the phone it easy enough to check. One of them called and looked at me and apologized. He told the others let's go. I said to him "would it take twelve officers to apprehend a sixteen year old?" He just looked at me, and said nothing. It was six cars, two officers in each car. You would think it was a raid of some kind. One of the other guys asked to use the phone. He wanted to call the nursing home to check on his dad's brother. No one had been to see him for sometime, and he had forgotten the phone number of the nursing home. When he got through his uncle had passed. I heard that it was really painful for him because they hadn't seen his uncle for sometime.

This reminded me of a dear friend of mine who had an aunt and uncle. Her aunt's name was Sarah. Sarah's husband's name was Benny. She wouldn't let anyone in her house, and Benny didn't like to stay home. He was retired, and would leave home for days. She still wouldn't let anyone in, not even to help her. She got sick, and no one knew about it for a week, when her husband returned home.

Her family wasn't allowed in her home either. When Benny got back from one of his weekend binges he took her to the hospital and would not return to check on her. She had no other friends and people were hesitant to visit her. Her only family was a sister and niece. They went to the hospital to see her. They told the hospital staff that they were family. When she came to herself, she asked them to leave. She just didn't want family around, but she would associate with outsiders, and even those that really didn't want to be bothered with her. She would even do all she could to help others.

While she was in the hospital, Benny continued to do what he wanted. He would bring his company home, because he had no freedom when she was in the house. Her sister, and niece were from out of town, and as soon as they got back home, she passed. They came back because they refused to act the way the sister acted. They refused to go to the house even though they were family. What a way to remember your sister. Things happen, and many times, you have no control over it.

Years ago, I remember my niece; her husband and family came to visit me when I was in West Virginia. As soon as they crossed this particular bridge it collapsed, and many people lost their lives. I was glad they were blessed to cross safely. I felt so bad for the ones that didn't make it. There were quite a few cars that went over the bridge. All the details were in the newspaper. A new bridge was to be built, but it hadn't happened at this time. This was such a tragedy.

There were men fishing from a boat not far from where the bridge had collapsed. I happened to know one of the guys fishing—he did not speak to his mother and father. He was thirty years old and thought, they were supposed to take care of him. He would catch large fish and give them away to other people.

I wonder what would cause a person not speak to their mother and father. You only have one of each. His parents had waited a long time to kick him out of the house. What he didn't realize was that after his mother and father, no one else would take care of him. I wonder how he thought someone owed him something. He didn't want to work to help himself. He was in the fishing boat when it almost turned over as the bridge collapsed. He was blessed that day because he had suffered no harm. The men usually drank liquor after fishing but he started before the fishing trip. The last I heard, he was a drifter, and still living wherever he could. I guess he still thinks the world owed him something.

14

How They Lived

There were two guys that went to school together outside the Paint Creek area; one white and one black, they were great friends. When you saw one, the other was always nearby. One night they stopped by a convenience market. They were known as Larry (black guy) and JC (white guy).

It just so happened, on this particular day that two other guys decided to rob a local market. The police were called. One of the policemen that showed up was JC's dad, he was the closest cop on duty. He did not tell the people that JC was his son. Larry and JC were at the store, but didn't have part in the robbery. The robbers didn't get any money, because, the owner had left earlier and taken the money with him.

There were only six people in the store. The policeman was trying to find out who was involved. The attendant was trying to implicate the black guy, but he was not responsible. They just happened to be in the wrong place at the wrong time. JC told her you know we were not here with these guys, the lady said I know you weren't, but what about him—referring to his friend Larry. JC said that Larry was with him. Neither of the guys had anything in their hands. JC told his dad if you take him, you have to arrest me too. He told the clerk, and you will have to testify, because we did nothing. Meanwhile, the clerk was trying to find out all about Larry, where he lived, his phone number and what he was all about, not paying any attention to the other guys.

The store attendant decided to drop all charges because the men never left the store with anything. JC talked her out of giving everybody a hard time.

Larry didn't visit his brother very much. He didn't approve of what he was doing. His wife worked and he didn't. He would have his friends in his home playing cards, smoking and drinking in the presence of his small children. Of course Larry couldn't do anything about it. He did however threaten to call child services, but he didn't want his brother to go to jail or the children taken away while their mother was at work. Eventually, the brother got careless and began to add players to the poker game. There was so much smoke in the house, one of the neighbors knocked on the door. They would not let her in, because they didn't want anyone to know what was happening inside the house. The neighbor thought there was a fire and she ran across the street, and called the fire department. The fire department was there before they could get the money and alcohol out of sight. They took the children out of that environment. The mother had to go to the trouble of getting her children back. After her husband explained what was going on, he had to move out and get a job. The mom had to find someone to care for their children so she could work. The good thing that came out of the situation is that the children were removed from that toxic environment.

At one time I lived near a couple that would drink excessively all the time. They had two girls; one eight, one ten. They even allowed the children to drink. Their reason being, if they drink at home they would know all about it. That really started a problem. By the time they became teenagers they were so hooked on the booze themselves that they would take what they had at home to school and give it to other students. They even started stealing money to buy booze. One teenager ran away and lived in her boyfriend's basement for two days. Her parents had to report her missing. When they went to work, she would go home and continue to steal things to pawn.

Eventually the teenager had to leave her boyfriend's house. He was afraid he would get in trouble. She got drunk, and fell down steps in her parents house, and hurt herself. They had to take her to the hospital. She had a broken wrist and sprained her ankle. They kept her there a week to get the alcohol out of her system and get her on the road to recovery. Children don't have to be taught bad habits, they will pick them up on their own. I often wondered what was the hurry to start drinking at such an early age, or at any age for that manner.

There was one guy that I went to school with, his dad married a woman that had two sons and one daughter. He also had a sister. He would tell us how nice the woman was before she married his dad. Soon after the wedding, she started treating him and his sister badly. If they asked their dad for something she would go around saying we don't have it. She didn't even talk to them like she would her own children. The woman and all the children were in the car together, and she was taking her daughter to band practice while yelling at her stepdaughter. She then got sick while behind the wheel and ran off the road. She thought she was having a heart attack, but it wasn't. She was the only one hurt. She had to go to the hospital and the family experienced a newfound freedom for two weeks. She was blessed to come out okay. She started acting better, but I suppose it takes time to change.

One evening a local family was eating dinner at a popular restaurant when the children became restless. There was also a white family at the next table with young children. One of the little boys turned his drink upside down. He was about three years old and was really restless. His parents looked at each other and said nothing. The waitress cleaned it up, and gave him more liquid to waste on the table, just because he kept yelling. People in the restaurant began to take note and glare at the family. As the young boy continued to show his unhappiness, his mother got up to go to the restroom. Another lady came out of the restroom, saying how embarrassed the mother was about her son's behavior. Neither parent even tried to correct the child. I suppose he needed someone to say no, just stop it. You can say no to your children and still love them.

Across town there was a robbery at a local convenience store. The owners didn't say much because they didn't want bad publicity for their business. One of the customers was leaving the store alone and was robbed of her purse. It was early in the evening, but still dark. The woman was knocked down and injured. By the time the police were called, the robbers were long gone. I think, I would have waited for the policemen to come outside, but sometimes we're not thinking to that end. There were bright lights outside, but that doesn't stop people when they want to do the wrong thing. It was a bad scene, because they had taken her car keys. I knew the lady, she had her checkbook, credit cards and other things taken She said the police opened the car door. She said no one offered their help. They just looked on.

This reminded me of a lady I once knew. She wouldn't offer anyone a ride. If she was asked, she always said I'm going the opposite direction. In her mind she thought she would never need anything. One of my good friends told me she had just finished shopping one morning and hit a truck side ways with a shopping cart while in the parking lot. Packages went in different directions. The groceries and other packages went all over the ground. People just looked at her and walked away. They were trying to tell her something. She needed help, but no one reached out to help her. I'm sure she understood what was happening. Someone that didn't know her stopped to help, but by that time, the wind had blown most of her stuff away. She just looked sad, but her attitude never changed. Some people are like that. Her children would make fun of other kids, that didn't have what they needed. They would laugh because they did not know better. They were just being children.

There was another guy, a senior citizen who lived nearby that always planted and maintained a large garden. He sold his vegetables to the local stores. People would take the vegetables and sell all that they couldn't use for themselves. This guy would give anything to anyone that wanted it. It made no difference to him.

Sarah had no family left and she was the last one of her generation. Sarah married a man that had grown daughters. Her husband died a few years after the marriage and she was left with the daughters. If they went to the grocery store, they would not let her get the food she wanted, and would get her what they wanted her to have as if she had no mind of her own. She knew they didn't want to be bothered with her.

I always tried to encourage Sarah, that things were not as bad as she thought, but they were. Why deny a person something they want to eat when they're paying for it. Sarah lived alone. Her stepchildren would take her around to pay bills and get whatever she had to have. Her stepchildren finally put her in a nursing home even though the lady was able to take care of herself. They just didn't want to help her. Her minister stepped up to help her and even her neighbors began to look out for her. After she got help, the stepdaughter left her alone. The last I heard, she was doing well.

There was a black lady I knew with a story similar to Sarah's. Her name was Jan. She went to live with her mother in her mother's house.

Her mother got sick and ended up in the hospital and later a rehab facility. First of all, she started changing her mother's house around, getting rid of her things without permission. Her mother had a small business, in one section of her house, because she was a seamstress. There were a couple of antique machines that people wanted to buy. There was also a lady that worked for her mother. She gave the lady two weeks to get rid of all the orders because she was closing up the place. She wouldn't allow the lady do what she could to keep things going. Jan even sold her mother's car. All this happened when her mother first left home. Everyone was surprised at her behavior because her mother was still of sound mind.

Before closing the shop, she got a loan on her mother's house, and never paid the bill. Her mother was in the rehab about a year, and she passed. Jan never paid the mortgage and the house was foreclosed on. Later on she got sick herself, and her children treated her almost as bad. They ignored her, and didn't come to see her, but once a year when they took their vacation. She went from the hospital to the nursing home. One of her dear friends wanted to keep her and take care of her. They said no. Her brother and his wife wanted to keep her it was still no. I wondered why it was such a big deal, when all she needed was a little help. Last I heard she was still in the nursing home.

A local policeman was running for mayor. He and his wife had four children. Two girls and two boys. The public knew his wife didn't treat the boys right. She made a difference in her own children. She would dress the girls nice, but she didn't care what the boys had on, and made them walk ahead of everybody else, as if they weren't a family. Neighborhood children would visit with the children talk about their visit and how the mom would treat the boys. The girls were six year old twins, and the boys were eight and ten.

The policeman did not get the job, because of how his wife treated their children. During one of his campaign meetings someone asked the question: why are your boys mistreated. He never answered. He just looked down and walked out of the building saying my friends let me down. One of his best buddies told him it wasn't your friends it was your wife. She never knew this would cost her husband the election. She really wanted to be a mayor's wife. She didn't break any laws; she was just a mean lady.

One morning, the two boys were playing in the neighborhood and wandered off in the woods and got lost. Police and others searched for them most of the night. The boys had stumbled upon a small cabin used by hunters when hunting overnight. They found snacks to eat and fell asleep in the cabin. They were found the next morning. Their mom was devastated because she was in fear of their lives; She had time to think about how it would have been, had they not been found. She cried when the boys were returned home, but it was more for relief than anything else. I'm told she didn't treat them much better after this event. It wasn't even a wake up call for her until they went to church on Sunday morning.

The church bus driver had stepped off the bus to help some of the passengers for just a few minutes when the eight-year-old boy jumped on the bus and took off. The bus was on the church lot and didn't stop before hitting about three cars as it crossed the highway and drifted into a garage and crashed. Everyone was amazed that the boy didn't hurt himself or anyone else.

One of the cars the boy hit belonged to a young married couple that came to church to laugh and make fun of others. They once told their next-door neighbors, that they were not living because they did not drink, smoke, or go to bars. In other words, you're not getting anything out of life unless you are doing these things. The couple wasn't so happy when their car was hit. They left before the police arrived because the car they had been driving belonged to someone else. The 8-year-old boy was released to his mother's custody. After this incident she had to take him to juvenile court and he had a curfew and community service.

You Reap What You Sow

In another section of town there were twin adult sisters—Sage and Page. I saw them a couple times. I didn't know what age they were, but they looked to be about thirty or thereabouts. Mark worked for the family for years doing odd jobs. From what I understood, he did almost everything that needed to be done around the house. Their mother had died and their father was sick. Only Page stayed around to see about her dad. The other daughter never showed up until he got very sick. When she received the word that her father was quite ill Sage came at once.

Her dad was very much alive, but very sick. His doctor made house calls so they kept him home. The guy that worked for them was named Mark. Mark was there when the twins grew up. As a matter of fact, he had worked for them most of his adult life. The family really depended on him.

Finally Gerald Anson passed and his daughter Sage wanted to know when and how much she would get. Mr. Anson had a farm, livestock, and insurance. Her sister got the house and Mr. Anson left an insurance policy for Mark, and he was to have a job as long as he was able. After the funeral service for her dad was over, Sage took her sister to court trying to get the house from her. She finally realized that what was in the will, was the way it would be. She never got anything more, and she left the lawyer's office and stopped speaking to her sister. Mark said that they don't even hear from her. Sage was never on the scene to give her father a drink of water. She never wanted to help out in any way. She was just out for what she could get. There are always those that want to help themselves to something belonging to someone else.

Close Encounters of the Wrong Kind

Jake, a young black man, and Ed, his friend, a young white man around the same age; enjoyed repairing houses and often did odd jobs together. Ed had a small shop with all kinds of tools. He would let people use the tools for a small fee, until they began to keep them instead of returning them back to the owner.

The two men purchased a couple of older large houses that needed repair and fixed them up for rental. It was on the order of a motel with no kitchen privileges. They would collect the rent once a month or every two weeks. Either Jake or Ed would do the collecting and all the tenants knew this.

One day Jake went to collect rent from one of the white tenant. He didn't have the rent, and made no effort to discuss the matter. As Jake began talking nicely, the tenant said just a minute and went inside, and came back with a gun. When Jake saw the gun, he knew then there would be no reasoning with this tenant and took off. The tenant shot at him twice.

When the police arrived the tenant was still talking about what no one was going to do. The police had to go inside to get him out of the room before he hurt somebody. They took the gun and he went to jail. After this incident, the owners established a place to drop the rent off because they decided, that it wasn't safe to collect from each individual. The owners kept the business for quite a while.

The other house they rented out was to a white couple. Both of them worked. They had two children. The daughter was a married adult and still living at home. She wouldn't keep a job, and kept borrowing money from her parents. They finally got fed up with this idea, and told her if she didn't get a job and pay it back, they would take her to court, but they never did. The daughter had her ten-year-old brother stealing from stores. She had him take things; he could put in his pockets like gloves, jewelry, makeup, etc.

The daughter also had a drinking problem and needed money. She would detain the clerk so that her brother could steal. They got by doing this for a while. One day her brother was out with another boy, and decided to take something for himself. He was caught, and put in a juvenile facility. It was in the papers, they didn't use his name because he was a minor. The neighbors knew who he was.

The parents blamed the daughter. She had taught him to steal. She knew it wasn't right and her brother was locked up. It should have been her. You don't get paid for stealing you get punished, so if it doesn't belong to you let it be, and move on.

I was having breakfast one day with a friend of mine that lived in a nearby community. Her brother came in the diner. He began to tell us about his neighbors. They were one of a kind. The whole family acted as if they were addicted to trouble. They seemed to follow in each other's footsteps. One of the oldest, around twenty-one, robbed a bank, one of the customers followed him outside. He dropped the bag and the money was blowing all over the place. The police had no problem catching him; they simply followed the money trail. Another one robbed a convenience store. He didn't get very much money. Two of them were trying to carry all the beer and cigarettes they could carry. They tied up the clerk, and went outside, and ran into a police car that was patrolling. He stopped to see what was going on. Both of them had two cases of beer, cartons of cigarettes and no car. No one else was in sight when the clerk yelled. Naturally the officer knew something was wrong. They didn't think to use a cart to carry their purchases out of the store.

Teenagers in the same family were stealing cars, and riding them around. One was sixteen years of age, and stopped for being behind the wheel of a stolen car. He ran into a parked car in a family's driveway trying to turn around. They were in the backyard, so they held him until the police came.

There were about eight siblings plus parents in that house. The ages ranged from teenagers to young adult. One brother and sister went into a loan company as a married couple to get a loan. They were trying to detain the manager, because it was lunchtime, and they knew he was alone. When they pulled a gun on the manager and asked for money from the safe he told them they didn't have money on hand during the lunch hour, when only one worker was available. If your loan was approved you would have to come back in an hour for the money. In the meantime, one of the workers called the manager to let him know they would be a few minutes late. The gunman let him talk, trying to listen to what was being said. When the manager said business was booming and he would take care of as many customers as possible. The other employee knew something was wrong, because they hadn't had a customer all day. The worker sent the police. The robbers were stupid enough to stay there with the gun. They didn't get any money, but they did get caught.

There were so many people in that house that the married couple should have moved out. They had two children that helped to keep the trouble going. For example, the married couple had two young children, and the adults were pouring alcohol in their cups.

A teenager was babysitting for them one night; the only difference is she was drinking the strong stuff. One of the young children somehow drank some liquor that was left in a glass on the floor. The child fell and cut her arm on the glass, and had to go to the hospital. Of course, the hospital called the police, and that was a wakeup call. They got tired of the investigation, and took better care of the children, because child protective service was always checking. I've never heard anything more about them stealing.

There were also two sisters that I went to school with; one of them I had not seen for many years. One sister lived with her parents, and didn't get along with them. In the house were the parents, a daughter, their brother and two grandchildren. The brother didn't want to help out in the family. Forty years of age and he thought he was supposed to live at his parent's house for free. It was the Ferris family. The son's name was Allen. The sisters were Neda and Astona. Astona was the one that lived at home. Actually, her parents were trying to help her. Every payday they had an argument. Allen would always say he was going to help with household expenses and then go out. When he returned home he would be broke. He wouldn't do the right thing and his family wouldn't put him out.

One afternoon he came home, and brought a friend of his. The family was about to sit down for dinner. I could hardly believe what he was about to tell me. Her brother went to the table before his mother and father as well as the others. In other words he was showing off. He asked his friend to come and have some dinner. Not knowing whether it was enough or not. Naturally his friend sat down. Of course he knew nothing of the circumstance surrounding this family. Allen resented his parents because he wanted to be the boss, but he never wanted to help pay for anything.

His dad was quiet until Allen's friend left. His dad approached him about the incident and they started arguing. The situation got out of hand. I suppose the father was tired of Allen's disrespect. A fight broke out between father and son. Allen ran for the gun, because he knew where it was. The gun went off and no one was hurt. His dad decided to call the police before someone got hurt seriously. The police got there before anything else happened. His dad stayed outside until they arrived. They took him, because he had the gun. His dad told police he didn't want him in the house anymore. He had really taken over his dad's house. When his dad took out a restraining order, he knew it was for real. His girl friend got him out of jail the next day. She let him live with her because his dad meant it. When he said he could not live with him anymore.

This situation turned out to be a disaster waiting to happen. Allen's girlfriend should have known that he wouldn't treat her any better because he didn't respect his parents. First of all, he had not gotten a job to pay her money back for bailing him out of jail. She let him drive her car. He had no license, and she knew that. He wrecked the car. When she told him what it would cost, without notice, he hit her with a broom. It brought blood from her face. She ran outside screaming. One of the neighbors called the police. She admitted letting him drive, but he was driving under the influence of alcohol. Allen went to jail for a second time. His girlfriend stopped helping him and decided to join the church, and make a better life for herself. He got two years and after that probation. I haven't heard anymore about her. Maybe it wasn't the place she wanted to be but it got her to the place she needed to be.

15

Life Lessons

I was visiting a church once with a friend of mine. One of the other ladies in the crowd was wearing more than her share of make-up. The minister said, I don't know how pretty you think you are because your beauty will fade in time. He wasn't talking about any specific person. I'm sure he never knew about her. She didn't take it very well, because she was talking about it after service, and it didn't sound good.

One day while listening to the inspirational channel when former football player Rosie Greir was talking about helping, and how it's a good thing, because you never know when you might need help yourself. He said it doesn't always have to be money. God blesses us and He knows where everybody lives.

Recently I ran into a lady that knew, a friend of mine from West Virginia named Rosalyn. I asked her about the family. She said you don't want to know. She had two children, but they had almost grown up when I saw them last. I just told her; I hope the news is good, but I wanted to hear about it anyway.

Her daughter Patsy brought a guy home that she had just met. After a short visit, he wanted to sleep over for the night. He had a car, they didn't know if it was his or not. They let him sleep over one night and he left when morning came, but the daughter went with him to help him find a job.

The guy's name was Mac. None of them knew anything about him. Mac said he was from Florida, but never said what city. They tried to help him. They were out for the evening, and Mac came by he said three times. He ended up breaking into the house. His reason for his action was he heard an intruder in the house and broke in to check the situation out.

The daughter didn't believe anything bad about Mac, but the family had no trouble until he showed up. Patsy's dad got Mac a room at a boarding house because he knew it wouldn't be the right thing to do—just to let him stay in their house. He was living at the boarding house and the lady in charge let him help around the place until he got a job at the furniture store. Patsy and her family were nice to him. When he got his first pay he took her to the movies and afterwards he dumped popcorn in her lap, and he said it was an accident.

Of course she never thought too much about it, until he bumped into one of the workers, and started a fight for no reason. Everyone around knew he was a troublemaker but her. It didn't end there, but he stopped by a convenience store on the way to her house, Patsy stayed in the car. He walked out of the store with the items he wanted without paying for them.

The clerk ran to the door, and saw him leaving. He knew Patsy, but had never seen her friend. Patsy didn't do anything but she was in the wrong place at the wrong time. Both of them were arrested, but he was at fault. She didn't know that he didn't have any money when he went into that store. She said I would have paid for it, and that the whole situation was simply nonsense, but this is what a troublemaker does, implicating others, when it isn't necessary. He had been to prison before so he really didn't mind. Patsy's parents got her out of the situation and Mac went to jail.

Patsy had a brother named Bob who was renting a house from one of the neighbors. He started letting other guys stay in the house to help pay the rent. The house had two bedrooms. Finally, there were four guys. They slept on the couch or wherever they could. Whenever one was gone, the other one would sleep in the bed. Bob had a place that they kept the money for the rent. No one knew, but the four of them.

One of the roommates had company and he decided to borrow from the rent money to finance the cookout. He made the mistake of getting the money while everyone was looking. His guests saw where he got the money from and as fate would have it the money vanished. When Bob found out what had happened, he suggested that his roommates pay for the loss. There was a hot disagreement and fight. Bob's roommates later called and said they would replace the money. They gave Bob a check and the check bounced. Again, Bob and his roommates got into a hot dispute and one roommate ended up in the hospital. Needless to say, this was the end of the relationship with the roomates.

Bob had a neighbor across the street that had about five dogs. His friend went away for a month, and promised to pay him a hundred dollars to take care of the dogs while he was gone. One of the dogs got sick and Bob didn't realize the dog was sick. The dog died. When his friend returned he was angry. He told Bob that he wouldn't get paid because he didn't take care of the dogs.

He took the neighbor to court, and won. He later decided that he would have to get a dog sitter or keep his own dogs. Rosalyn told me he always kept a couple guys around to help pay his rent.

One of my neighbor's daughters was in a bridal shop trying on a dress for her wedding. The girl's future mother-in-law who happened to be with her didn't want the wedding to take place even though she had no real complaint against her son's fiancee. She complained about everything and was a real downer to be around. The wedding took place anyway. Finally, the mother-in-law began to tell people it shouldn't have happened. There wasn't anything she could do because the bride and groom were of age. In fact, she showed up thirty minutes late for the ceremony. She just wanted to humiliate her daughter in-law to be.

The mother-in-law didn't do what she had committed to do with regard to the wedding. She was in charge of refreshments. After trying to knock the punch bowl over, she fell and hurt herself. She was laid up for a couple of weeks. Who do you think was there for her? Her daughter in-law, in other words, you never know when you will need help, or who will be willing to help you.

Gus was a very nice man that the community loved. He managed to get a boys and girls softball team organized. The young people and most of the parents were excited about the team. The youth would clean the building and grounds and Gus would oversee the operation. Any money raised would be for activities, uniforms, equipment and the children's entertainment.

One day, one of the boys was pitching, and his dad was there when he lost the game. The dad became upset, went out on the field and started trouble. He and Gus had words and he began to talk about Gus around the neighborhood. He was actually jealous, because he never came up with the idea for the children. Gus told him he could take over. He never wanted to help. He just wanted to be in control. His son was ten years old and embarrassed by his father's actions, but he never quit the team because it was great fun, and gave him something to do.

There was a retired police detective in the same neighborhood named Mr. Chase. He was kind to everyone, especially the children. He was at a roadside cafe when a guy on a motorcycle hit a little girl. She was out riding her bike. Her mother was inside the store. The child was taken to the hospital. The hospital found out there was no insurance.

Mr. Chase began at once trying to raise money to help with the hospital bill. The guy that hit her went to jail. Mr. Chase went to every business establishment he could and placed containers for contributions to help with medical expenses. The money was really coming in, because everyone knew how medical bills could escalate. One couple in the neighborhood didn't give anything and accused Mr. Chase of taking part of the money. Chase didn't handle any of the money and no one paid any attention to the couple, because the people knew his reputation. He just always tried to help other people. It's a great thing to help others, because you never know when the four-letter word "h e l p" will come your way. He would ask people to donate when they bought gas or even shopped at the store. He challenged the accusing couple to donate and they refused. He also proved that he never touched the money because there were witnesses when he was around the money. There is always someone that doesn't want the program to go on.

Children on the Loose

I went to the doctor's office out of town with a friend of mine. While I was there a black lady came in with three youngsters. Did they ever make a scene? The lady said hi and I said hi. I made the remark. "No school today." The oldest one said: "I'm sixteen, and I don' t have to go, if I don't want to. Then I found out the other ones were thirteen and fifteen.

The lady said I'm their aunt and they don't go half the time. I asked the oldest one, how would you get a job? She said I don't need a job, I'm getting married. I did say, but you're not old enough.

I suggested that they could work at McDonald's after school. The 16 year old replied they don't pay enough money. I said, "you all have a great aunt, but you have to go to school because the officials will call or come to your door. School is in session, and you must go."

You all are lucky if no one has been in touch with you. Before we left a patient came in. He thought the teenagers were there for treatment. He remarked: I wish you strong young guys would come and help me in the evenings after school. He had a huge farm. There were vegetables and fruit to be picked. They laughed as if the word "h e l p" was a dirty word.

The children's aunt got his phone number, but first she had to deal with them going to school. When I left, I said I hope everything works out for you. I told the children, if I never see you again get back in school. You will be glad you did one day. Hopefully they listened, but there are no guarantees.

Across from the doctor's office was a school. As we walked outside one of the boys around six or seven years of age, threw a baseball bat at his mother. I just assumed it was his mother, because she came to pick him up, and he wasn't ready to go home. Someone said he talked to her something awful every time she came around. Being just a kid, a little discipline was what he needed. She didn't do anything to stop him so there will be another opportunity to convince him that this isn't the way to act.

I knew of a mother who said she couldn't do anything with her children. The grandmother took them and I understand that she was given permanent custody. The neighbors said their grandmother didn't send the children, but she took them to Sunday school and church and kept them in school. She wouldn't let them stay home unless they were sick, and she threatened to take them to the doctor. After that it was a way of life for them.

The children finished high school and began to make a better life for themselves. They loved their grandmother for stepping in, because her help was very much needed. I heard she got the job done, just teaching them what they should have been doing in the beginning.

Schemes Galore

This reminded me of what happened on one street I lived. At one time I heard police sirens. I walked out on the porch to see what was going on. It was a black guy and a white lady. He came to the door talking loud so that everyone could hear him. To me they were known as Vince and Jodi Loder very nice neighbors. He told the police she took all of his money, and didn't leave him any. I thought they were a happy married couple.

He told the police she doesn't work, and she's not my wife. The police asked if they were roommates Vince said no she just takes my money. He had put her out of the house, but he wasn't supposed to do that, because she lived there too. She really wanted to leave at that time to go to her mother's. That ordeal had the attention of everyone that passed.

In the meantime, Jodi had a friend who was coming to visit. A cab drove up, and she got out. She came in on the greyhound bus. I'm sure she was aware that something was wrong. This was so unusual. Jodi had to take her friend inside of Vince's house. He continued to talk loud, and told the police, he would not make another scene if they left, and that he would take part of his money. She had taken it all. I couldn't see if she gave up part of the money. I imagine she did because they were quiet after the police left. Jodi found out that her friend had stole some money from a greyhound bus station where she worked. She came all the way from the small town where she lived in Virginia. She had the money in a locker in the small town where she left. She told Jodi, that she would help pay for rent and food, but she didn't know that the situation with the couple she had come to visit was so intense. She just wanted to stay around Jodi until she heard some word concerning the money.

Jodi's friend was called "Babs." She was supposed to be on vacation. In fact she just wanted to be gone, when the money was missing so it wouldn't lead to her.

Vince let both ladies stay, because Babs was agreeing to help with expenses. He heard her say, that she wanted to stay around and get a job, so he welcomed the idea. A week later the company missed the money. She called home, and one of her friends told her what had happened, and all the employees were questioned. Her friend didn't know about the money. The newspaper reported that thirty five hundred dollars was missing. She had already started spending the money. After two weeks, Babs got a job at a diner. Vince could hardly wait to get the extra money, so he could have more to spend.

She worked about a month, when she got paid; she didn't give Vince any money. Jodi told me both of them were going back to Babs' hometown because she wanted to get rid of Vince anyway. They left when he was at work on the greyhound bus, because Babs could ride free anyway.

She thought about staying with Vince, but when she went back home she figured she could use Jodi's name if something came up about the money, especially if both women were working. When Vince came home, sure enough, both ladies were gone and there was no money for Vince. Not even in the bank.

She went back to her job, and went through the questioning as the other employees. The company had no proof, as to where the money was. Babs made the mistake of taking Jodi out to dinner twice in one week while she was not working. Babs worked at the bus station during the day, and she had no business there at night. One night she went back to the terminal to get some of the money. She saw a couple of workers, and she didn't go to the locker. I was told that Jodi went back home, and sent Babs the next day. It looked better for a stranger to have a locker at the bus station.

Jodi didn't know she was going for money. She just took the key, but when she reached for the paper bag she dropped it, because it was not together. She took it from the locker. It was the busiest part of the day.

A couple of people saw her. There she was in the wrong place at the wrong time. One of the workers took her to the boss instead of the police. Babs' boss found out Jodi was a stranger in town. She told him where she stayed and he put it all together. She got off easy. He told her if she paid the money back, he wouldn't prosecute her. There wasn't very much money involved, but it didn't belong to her. She had to pay it back, and then she got fired.

This reminds me of what a customer did when we were in the grocery store in line together. This lady that I did not know started talking to me, she had a bag with something in it, and she was eating whatever was in the bag. I noticed the manager kept looking at us. I knew who he was because I went to this particular store all the time. She was in front of me so I was about to see what was going to happen because I wasn't guilty. She had been eating grapes, but I didn't understand why she had a can of corn down in the bag of grapes. It didn't make sense to me. She told me she was going to pay for it, and wondered why he was still watching her. She left the can of corn on the counter, but she had eaten the grapes. He called her aside as we were talking; I never knew she had a can of corn. I made sure she didn't put it in my groceries. When I left the store she was still there. I was told he had her pay for the grapes, and asked that she shop elsewhere from now on.

This reminded me of what happened at an all you can eat restaurant where I was dining. Four ladies were together. I noticed that one white lady had an exceptionally large bag, it was not a purse, and she kept putting food in this bag, and no one said anything. The staff ignored the fact that this lady had all this food. They were watching a black couple, that didn't take anything, at least when I was there. First of all, the black lady's daughter worked there, and they had all the food they needed because she was allowed to take leftovers home. It was interesting to see how the situation was playing out. The white lady with the large bag now loaded with food ended up walking out of the restaurant without even being approached.

Two young men joined a small church. A friend of mine, that was a member of that church, said their intentions weren't good. They only wanted access to the church. Soon after joining they volunteered to clean the church for free. One of the men was not working at the time. One night after service, the guys announced that they would clean the church a little later. Everyone else cleaned in the daytime. After church was over, and everyone went home, one the deacons got suspicious, and turned around and went back to the church. The deacon was parked out of sight. The guys had left church along with everyone else but after about an hour they came back to the church with a flashlight. It had gotten dark and they were walking with the flashlight on, because all the lights were off around and close to the church building. The men entered the church and were in there for probably less than an hour when they came out carrying two large bags. One of them dropped the bag he was carrying. As soon as this happened they looked up and into the deacon's eyes. The men were in the process of stealing from the church—that was embarrassment, and then some. The deacon told them to take the equipment back, and never come around again. They got a break and didn't go to jail, this time but that doesn't always happen, because taking something that doesn't belong to you is asking for trouble.

Family Drama

Ada and her mom's boyfriend didn't get along. He killed her dog as soon as Ada's mom let him move in, so they never got along, and when she resisted his advances, he started lying on her. He was telling her friends she was after him. Her friends and the entire neighborhood knew better.

Ada moved out of her mother's house to let everybody know she couldn't stand him. Fred just wanted to make trouble for both of them. He told her mother he wanted to marry her, but he was saying this just to start a family dispute. Fred didn't care about her, because he had another girlfriend. This lady's name was Shannon. She was a very nice lady that attended church. Fred knew she was not taking foolishness from him. He would even go to church with her. He had no intention of marrying anyone. He wasn't serious. When he didn't go to church with Shannon—I was told he would try to look in the windows, or sneak in and look around in church to see what she was doing. What a guy, he just wasn't serious about anyone or anything, and as far as I knew he never married anybody.

One night Shannon went to church and when she returned home, Fred jumped on her. They had a big fight, and one of her neighbors called the police, when they saw what was going on. Of course she pressed charges, and that was the end of their relationship, because it wasn't going to get any better.

The way that Fred was treating Shannon reminded me of an old friend of mine that I ran into at an out of town church. Dan was nice to his wife, but mistreated his mother-in-law. I was told about the situation, but this was my first time to be at the scene of what was happening.

Outside the church he was helping her into the car, and yelling. He said, I know there is nothing wrong with you, and you can do more to help yourself. His wife said they argue all the time. I know she was embarrassed, but I suppose she couldn't do much about it. It would only make matters worse especially in public. He didn't realize that he would need help someday.

Mercy and Change of Heart

Dan worked as a security guard on the midnight shift. It was a restaurant and bar combined. Just after his shift was over, he was shot trying to break up somebody else's fight outside. He was in the hospital for a couple of months. Finally he was out of the hospital and in a wheel chair, and had to go to therapy for quite sometime. At a young age, he never thought he would need help.

Fred also reminded me of this schoolteacher. Mrs. Allen that had two sons, Brad and Dave, and one daughter Jane. The guys were always around to help mom, because their dad left town before they became school age. Now that they're all grown up Jane was leaving home. She was almost eighteen. The family didn't hear from Jane for a couple of years. She was working at a grocery store. She carried a large purse and it was later discovered that she was stealing the things she needed. She had been on this job about a month. Her boss liked her work. She was always on time. The lady she lived with gave her a good recommendation. I couldn't believe what I was hearing.

She told Jane the boss knows what you're doing at work. You know they will put you in jail. Jane was company to her, and she wanted her to stop stealing, she had been trying to help her every since she had been there. She talked to the people at the store, and they said she could stay if she stopped stealing.

As her landlord talked to her, she decided to quit taking things, because Ashley her landlord paid for the things she took, which wasn't worth it. It was candy, a jar of coffee, or make-up. Things she could do without. No one needed to tell her if she continued to steal, she would eventually get caught. She changed because her landlord was trying to help her.

There was a black couple in the same neighborhood, the Swansons, with a nineteen-year-old son named John, and a sixteen-year-old daughter Julia. The daughter had a boyfriend that was a nice church going guy. In fact his whole family were churchgoers. Can you believe that her family didn't want her to go to church, and have a better life, so they gave her an ultimatum, if you are going to church with him, go over there and live. Her family knew that this was not going to happen. She was only sixteen. Her family was responsible for her well being, and they knew this. They didn't like John; her family didn't want him for a son in law because they couldn't manipulate him. Julia's mom was always asking John to pick up alcohol and cigarettes so that she would have something to talk about and embarrass him in public, but John didn't fall for it, and he never brought her anything. The lady wasn't even ashamed as she tried to lure this young man from the church. She should have been going herself, and taking her own family.

Two years later the couple got married because Julia. After the couple married Julia's mother started going to church, and to my understanding, she continued, and eventually her whole family started following her. You never know when you do the right thing that it might encourage someone else, and that's a good thing.

16

Grace and Mercy

I was out of town not long ago and had a chance to talk to a minister Perry and his wife. He was speaking to students at a middle school. He was telling me what I already knew, as he was trying to encourage the younger generation. He told them to hold on to what they believed in, and stay out of trouble. He told the parents to encourage their children, because it is time to come to the Lord, and bring them with you, and do all you can for the Lord. This minister was telling them some of the incidents that happened in his hometown. A few teenagers were racing each other in cars. They were drinking and going so fast that the car went up a pole and turned over. They came out with minor injuries. The Lord was with them. The police couldn't understand how they escaped death. Only God knows, but He keeps doing great things for us.

The teenagers thought this was funny, because they missed the curb. The thing about it is that someone else could have been killed. The impact alone could have killed them. No one said, thank God, because that's the reason they survived, even though they never realized it. Would you believe they enjoyed the ride, and made silly comments, like next time we will race in a bus, and take more people. That was kind of sad, acting as if they had nine lives.

The Lord is just good. One day He will say well done, but not if you haven't done anything. Satan is ruthless. He will attack you, your family, the home and whatever is nearest and dearest to you. We need God's help so that we can fight for the welfare of our homes, church, community and nation. In fact, he would take over, but for the grace of God. The greatest threat to Satan's kingdom is total commitment to spreading the good news of the gospel of peace. He is the cause of sin and strife in the world, but we oppose him in a peaceful manner.

You don't have to have a dreadful or terminal disease, and you don't have to be old to die. Death will certainly be there ready or not. He is not your friend. The devil has two things to say, you have plenty of time, and its too late. He doesn't care about anyone.

There was another family that lived not far from me at one time. They were the Hodges; they had two sons and one daughter. Mr. Hodges would take his older son everywhere he went. He was even seen out in the nightlife. I was told they acted like brothers. One night his son Jim was driving his car, and hit another car. His dad had just asked him to slow down. He didn't listen, because he didn't want to do what his dad had said. He was too old to have a whipping because he was an adult. He didn't even realize that he was supposed to honor his father and mother. At this time, he didn't need a buddy, he needed a friend, but he didn't want it to be his dad. Dad and son, family ties, whatever happens they will always be dad and son that will never change.

Had he not been drinking, he wouldn't have to go to jail. Jim would not say I'm sorry. After the police came on the scene, he still wouldn't say I'm sorry. It's so funny how people will do something nice, like taking you to dinner, or buy a gift, rather than say I'm sorry. His dad did not need him for a buddy in the first place. In this same town where a minister was having church service there was a guy in the audience that didn't particularly care for him. He just walked almost to the pulpit, and shot him at close range. The guy that shot him went to jail, but got out of it because it was only a flesh wound, and the wounded guy never pressed charges. What an unusual case. It's almost as if this never happened.

This minister was trying to help others, and do something useful for the church. It's a good thing when you take the time to help someone. Almost everybody is on a time schedule. Some people may want you to write a letter, or others may need someone to run an errand. You could be on your way to work, thinking about the time you spent in the traffic, and then there's quiet time. At this time it gives you the opportunity to pray.

It's God's gift to you for the moment, a day at a time, sleep consumes a large amount of your time. We must remember when our time runs

91

out we're in big trouble if we don't have God on our side. As you begin to do the right thing, God will open doors of greater service and responsibility, without hesitation, you will be doing greater things. The Lord doesn't expect you to do everything, but He does expect us to do what He tells us to do.

Every day is precious, because time is winding up and time is valuable in the Christian service of the Lord, and doing something useful for the Master's use. You would be amazed to know who will not listen to gospel programs on TV, and who makes fun of people that are trying to serve God. If anyone needs your help and prayers, you should give it, with full speed ahead. You can't do too much for God considering what He has done for us.

One man's blood saved the nation and the whole world from sin. We need to study God's word at all times. There is no reason for not doing so. It is not optional, it's required reading.

A true friend is one that you can go to for comfort, encouragement, and understanding.

Christians today have an advantage. We have the scriptures to guide us, and the Lord to open up our understanding.

We are blessed to have bibles in our homes today. They are often used to preserve mementos, or family history, instead of fulfilling their God given purpose. Misuse leads to neglect, and in essence the bible becomes a lost book among a growing number of families. We should keep it before our eyes and hide its contents in our hearts.

I know of a minister outside of Paint Creek who was the pastor of a church. He already had a wife, and three grown children, and even grandchildren. He left his wife, and started another family. Last time I heard about him, he was still inviting people to church. People in the community knew his history. New members did not stay in the church when they found out what was happening. It's no surprise that the church didn't prosper. God is not in the midst of confusion. The pastor denied the allegation, but the facts remain the same. Sin is sin and one is no greater than the other.

Sometime we treat God's promises as if they're not real. Some have doubts of God's ability or desire to follow through. When we won't trust God for help, we are left to depend on others and ourselves. Since we are painfully aware of human limitations, we worry about the present, the future and eternity. All we have to do is trust in God.

We should build our lives on a strong, spiritual foundation, so we can withstand the physical and emotional peril that will arise. That strong foundation is Jesus. The Holy Spirit is at work today, just like the wind, we can't see him but the results of his activity has been manifested.

Our lives may be different, but we can encounter circumstances that ravage our physical and emotional well-being. We can have problems, that take our strength. Society is filled with enticing options that limit our spiritual growth and happiness.

There was a minister that was going from door to door who told us, when it comes to being saved, most people want to talk, and not listen. Those who grow up in a Christian environment should not be shocked by the real world. The evil is offensive, but even more distressing is the double standards of Christians who use their strength to praise God on one hand and on the other hand influence people negatively. We are to spread the gospel message, and bring hope and encouragement to suffering people. It sometimes calms the excited and causes the unruly to be quiet.

Through it all, God is good. He's the only one that can help us overcome, and conquer the enemy. There are so many souls out there that think it isn't necessary to assemble themselves in God's house. They get saved, and have no intentions of changing their habits, because you really have to learn how to live a clean and wholesome life.

We start by obeying those in authority. We should have no problem obeying the law, that's a must. Why give the church a hassle?

I was visiting another church one Sunday. One of the members came in the restroom where I was, and started asking all kinds of silly questions like who are you? Where did you come from? She really wasn't very friendly. I just ignored her silly statements. Sometime people let every little thing said in church upset them. This is just an excuse not to come back. Some people really don't want to be in church anyway. Every individual should be there for his or her own benefit.

Getting back to my visit to the church; having just ignored the lady that had asked me who I was and where did I come from. A second woman came behind the first and asked the same questions; this added insult to injury. What a way to greet the visitors.

As a visitor I had come to church that morning to hear the Word of the Lord and to fellowship with other Christians. Thank God for giving us the Holy scriptures, which inform us of all we need to know from beginning to the end.

Many people desire wealth and luxury, even if acquired at the expense of others. Some are fortunate, and yet unwilling to share, or sacrifice for others. Human nature finds it difficult to accept the Christian concept of forgive and forget. The Lord has given mercy to all of us. Some people may harm another unknowingly, but we are not to seek revenge. That is another clever tactic of the devil to defeat everyone. He wants us to follow him away from God.

Let us enjoy our life as God strengthens our faith, and brings us closer to Him. The Lord wants us to do our best in all our daily tasks and in his service. Accepting God's word in sincere faith, we may be confident, that He will bless our endeavors in His own way.

17

Family and Friends

I took the time a couple years back to visit my niece and her husband. in Florida. My sister Odessa and I met there the same day. My flight was about forty-five minutes earlier. From the time we got there, it was nothing but fun at their house. We went sightseeing every day, and the weather was about 80 degrees, there was bible study and church on Sunday; and eating out. There are many ministers in my family. We even visited the Holy Land. After this visit I went to see my grandson and his wife Anthony and Jessica in Georgia. This was a fun trip also. All I had to do was rest and enjoy the baby until we went out to eat and sightsee. The other two kids were out of town. I was treated like royalty at both houses. They're family anyway.

There are many ministers in my family. My nephew has a church in Brandon, FL. We held a family reunion there and the members were so kind to us. My thanks also to all those that prayed for my son William (Billy) during his illness. I also have a grandson that recently started a church in Hamilton, Ohio. They are both doing very well.

My time was limited while in Florida because I wanted to come home and check on my son. When I got home not much had changed. In my estimation he was still struggling and hanging on to life. I was there almost everyday, sometimes twice. The only time that I missed, was when I wasn't feeling well myself.

I have great friends in Delaware. I actually have two homes away from home, C. Bohanna, and the Kimbro family. When I'm in Delaware, I don't need a hotel. I just go to either house. I'm normally there about once a year or whenever I'm in town.

A Long Illness

My son William (Billy) was sick for two and a half years. It started with a heart attack. Later he had to have a pacemaker, then a trachea tube. This kept him from talking. There were times after surgery when he would be connected to many tubes, ventilators and etc. The doctor said don't be alarmed at what you see, his vitals are fine, and he's okay. From that day on he was moved from one hospital to another, to the rehab center and back. He would do well for a while, but there were always problems. I would visit him in rehab one day, and he would be walking. I would go another day, and he would be in bed. After he was in bed for a few days, I would ask if someone would please get him up to move him.

It is not easy to watch a loved one suffer and believe me, he had his share. He was brought from the hospital where he had his surgery. The first thing I noticed was a tube in his nose for feeding. I began by asking if the tube could be placed elsewhere. He had to have it in at that time, but it still didn't make me feel any better.

I once had a hospital stay which resulted from a fall. A tube was placed in my throat for about three hours to check my stomach. It's a horrible experience. I went through this with him. He was the one with the pain and suffering. I was thinking about the medication he had to take. At this time, the food and medicine had to go through the tube. At this point I began to call family and friends to pray for him. When he left the first hospital to go to the rehab I found out he had diabetes. I watched for a period of time, the wear and tear on his body. I knew someone that had dialysis and went on to live for years but wasn't in his condition.

I remember in the facility, he was in before dialysis; I would go and sit for hours, because he was always asleep. One morning, I got there around eleven, and I didn't leave until five thirty. He was asleep all that time until I woke him up. I knew he was supposed to wake up at some point.

I began to ask questions, to find out why or if he was medicated. I knew he wasn't supposed to sleep all the time. I was just trying to find out how responsive he was. He lay there day after day not getting any better. I just wanted the best for my son, and to do all that I could to help him. He went through things that I couldn't even imagine. So many times he was not aware of what was going on around him. I was sitting there one day talking to another lady that said she had a problem, but her problem was not sickness. She had a friend she was living with and she had no money to pay her.

As soon as she got on her feet, so to speak, she went to live with somebody else; that happens. As she was telling me her story, a white minister came in, that always prayed for my son. I really don't remember his name, and I'm sorry, but he always stopped by his room. I'm so glad he did, and I thank God for him, because he would pray for all the patients.

I always knew when my son William was not feeling well, but what I really don't understand is through it all, I never heard him complain. I have never seen anyone suffer like this. He would lay there not moving. I could hardly stand it. All I could do was sit there.

He liked the quietness; you might say he was a loner. Sometimes I had to be sure he was okay, because he always wanted to be alone. All he wanted to do was go to work and back home. He served in the armed forces and worked for Indian River School Correctional Institute for twenty years before he became ill.

Many days I went to see him and left hurting because I couldn't help him. The idea came to me that he should be moved elsewhere for evaluation.

In my mind, I believed a change would be good for him. At that time it didn't take place. It was about four weeks later and he began to get some better; he was more alert; but the problems remained. The ones in charge medically didn't exactly agree to a change at this particular time so he had to remain at the same facility another month. Finally, he was moved to another location. When he was responsive, he would clap his hands when I came around. He was probably just looking for someone in the family. When he didn't like the menu he would not eat.

Sometimes, family members would bring him whatever he desired to eat; with permission of course.

When he started dialysis, I would attempt to explain to him how important it was, but I'm sure he already knew. Sometimes, after a dialysis session, he would be so sick and wet with perspiration that the rehab center would send him to the hospital.

I would be at the hospital almost daily, checking on him. making sure that he was getting the assistance he needed. We communicated pretty good because he would write on a piece of paper what he wanted me to know. He would write a couple of words, and I knew what he was trying to say. As he got worse, he would watch me as I moved around the room as if to say, help me.

As I talked to him, I would try to maintain my own composure and assure him everything would be all right. One day the nurse was checking his sugar. His finger started bleeding so she had to put a band-aid on it. It was hard for me just watching. He lay there calm as usual, better than I would because I hate to see anyone stuck with a needle. That's pain from the beginning. Someday, I hope the medical field will find a better way.

I thank God for the health and strength that allowed me to go and be there for him. It was a blessing to be there; even when he wasn't aware that I was present.

It's no fun going in and out of rehab or the hospital, but that's life. He was in three different hospitals and two rehab centers. He went from one to the other for two years and eight months. After his heart surgery, he never had a chance to return home.

I wanted to get him out of there for a couple of hours, just for a change of scenery. It never happened. I felt so sorry for him when the holidays came and passed and he would spend them at one of the facilities. I always had to go, and see if he was all right. I miss him, he was a nice guy, never hurt anyone. Anything he did was to himself. He was always trying to help others.

I always watched him in pain, when he was waiting for some sort of medication. Whenever I would ask him if he was in pain, he was most of the time. It never got any better as the wear and tear of his heart and the dialysis took a toll on him as well as high blood pressure; sometimes it was low blood pressure. It was always one thing or another that kept him going almost every week from rehab to the hospital.

In rehab, William had a couple of nice roommates. Dino was his friend and the Milini family. Their kindness was uplifting to him. Another roommate was K. Lassiter. His wife Shirley was always doing something nice to help William. I always appreciated anything anyone did for him. Anytime a person is confined it's a good thing to wave at them or just say hi. I treated everyone nice, even the people that I didn't know, because it is the thing to do.

I was in a store nearby the rehab to get a cold drink for myself when a very nice young lady asked me if she could help me find something. She wasn't even a worker. I thank God for her, and I pray that she will always be blessed, because she didn't have to do it. It really made my day to run into someone so nice.

We have another great friend. I will call D.J. which has always been a blessing, praying and helping my son in many ways. I appreciate, and thank God for having a true friend like her. Thanks for being there. I shall always treasure your friendship. Not only did you help my son William and family in so many ways, but also you keep on doing great things. God bless you and your family. I love all of you. You are the kind of friend that you don't have to ask for help. Thanks for everything and all that you do.

You never know when sickness will come to your door, and it will. It is good to treat people as you would like to be treated and do unto others as you have them do unto you, because you will need mercy. I just wanted the best for my son as he suffered and endured this awful pain and suffering. I tried not to think about all the complications he was experiencing. Then I began to hear about the many change happening in his body.

I had a sister that was diabetic. She had to take insulin. They would give her different tests when she went to the hospital. I knew she had her share of pain and suffering also, but she was never connected up to any medical devices. I was visiting her once. We were going out for breakfast and I rushed to get ready. It wasn't a problem for me. I was younger and not sick. I said you're not ready yet? She said keep on living. What she meant was time will bring about a change.

Every time I went to the rehab center, and the ambulance was outside. I couldn't get inside fast; I always thought it was there for William. He was in the hospital so much of the time.

Many times I went to rehab early; not knowing he was in dialysis. It made absolutely no difference to me. Dialysis takes about four hours. I would sit and wait for him. Most of the time he would have to go to the hospital afterwards because he would end up with an awful temperature. I would sit there until his temperature would subside.

I left him one evening at the rehab center, and as soon as I got home, I got a call, that he was taken to the hospital. I would get up getting ready to see about him. This was one habit that was hard to break. I knew I couldn't do anything, but I wanted to be there to see what was going on with him. Hoping and praying that he would have a good day. He really was a nice guy. So many times when his nephews and nieces came to see him, you would see a big smile on his face. They always wanted to visit him.

He had to lie in bed day after day. I would hear the phrase this or that wouldn't help him. I was willing to try anything that would give him comfort or save his life. He often would not ask for medication. One of the staff would ask him, if he needed anything, then he would say yes, or nod his head.

Now I know how my neighbor at one time felt, when someone shot her son. I saw his sister outside talking to the other brother. I knew his sister, but I had never seen him before. I just walked across the street to talk to her. I asked his sister Candi if he was the youngest brother. He said no all loud and nasty. She stopped him right there, and told him, she just asked, she doesn't know you. It was nice of her to intervene for his rudeness.

It's sad when a person has no regards for another's feelings. They're not thinking about "do unto others as you would have them do unto you," because that's what will happen.

It's hard to think about it, William never got off the ventilator completely. Sometimes he was off for two or three hours at a time. I would whisper into his ear and tell him to pray, because I couldn't imagine what he was going through. I knew all along that only God could help him.

Christmas day he was on a regular diet. Through it all, he would always eat. I would help him, but he could do it himself. I didn't get too close to him, because I didn't feel well. I thought it might be a cold or something. That same day one of his brothers fed him. He ate all of his food.

This was on Tuesday afternoon. I asked my daughter and other family members to check on him on Wednesday. I didn't go, because I wasn't feeling well. I missed one day. I went out to see him on Thursday. He had a feeding tube in his nose. I knew this was uncomfortable, that's why I was trying to get it removed to the stomach like I knew he wanted to eat. He was asking for food. I always carried a pencil and paper, so whenever he was able he would write what he wanted me to know. The last word he wrote to me was "snack", that meant he was hungry. I couldn't feed him, and that really hurt me, because he had that tube in his nose, and being feed through the tube. Evidently it was not enough because he was still hungry. It hurt me just having him ask for food and water and we could only give him ice.

He was sick from dialysis that day. I had been there about an hour and a half so I had to leave for a while. As he tried to get out of bed, he could move around at times on his own. I went back a couple of hours later. He was wet with perspiration, but he knew who I was. I went to his nurse to find out what was going on with him. She said we are sending him to the hospital. I'm doing the paper work as we speak.

The next day, my daughter called and told me that there were so many family members there that I didn't need to go, but I had a weary feeling. I didn't go out at all that day. The second trip I made on Friday was the last time I saw him alive.

My daughter came in about eleven forty that night and told me what I already knew; William had passed. I knew he would not get over all the things that he was plagued with, but I didn't think it would happen at that time. No one wants their family to leave them, but God knows when and what to do. I'm so glad He is in control. I just want to thank everyone that said or did anything to help him. If you weren't there, or you said a prayer I thank you. Time is something that you can't get back, and you do not know how much you have.

Pastor Moore and Pastor Kim Strain and the Outreach Ministries both of Delaware prayed and sent cards throughout Billy's illness.

I have many friends that prayed for my son. I know I can't mention everyone by name, and if I missed a name I should have written I'm sorry and thank you anyway, and may God bless you. Elder A. Walker visited and prayed for my son William when he first got sick, and would still be at the church on time to teach the adult Sunday school class. He was there from the beginning of his illness to the end.

Elder Walker was always there for William. His wife C. Walker would always call to see about him as well as pray for him. I am so grateful how the Lord blessed me to go and check on him. Sometime he had a great day, and doing fine. Other times, he was not feeling well, but I thank God for the good times because, time was on his side for two and a half years in sickness. I'm thankful he's in God's hands.

18

Speaking of Churches

Speaking of churches, Apostolic Faith Assembly Church of Canton, OH was built from the ground up under the supervision of Pastor Barbara Winn. Pastor Winn was a high school teacher, wife, mother and pastor. She was the first black woman I ever knew or heard of to take on a task of this magnitude. She built the church from tithes and offerings, with no sales. It's unusual for a woman pastor to accomplish so much in such a short period of time, or even in a lifetime.

Pastor Winn was a great lady. I had the privilege of knowing her. What I liked the most about her was that every time I went to church or whenever I saw her, she was always the same. Just being her nice friendly self and on time for all services. When you went to the church you felt welcomed and wanted to go back. I remember her saying that she would speak to people, move on and not look back to see if they spoke to her or not, especially when people are a respecter of person. She always had something helpful to say. I never heard anything but good things about her. Pastor Winn practiced what she preached. She was a true Christian in every sense of the word. I was so inspired by her lifestyle and her Christian walk. She had a lot of wisdom even though she was young.

The congregation grew fast under her leadership, partly due to the simple presentation of the Gospel to the lost. The lady was just phenomenal. It was a great loss when she went home to be with the Lord.

I ran into an old high school buddy of mine named Corine, while on the plane to Orlando, FL. She had met a pastor in one of the small churches in the area and was going there to support him in a revival.

This was a very nice thing to do. Doing something to support someone else. Corine's mind was headed in the right direction. The pastor was also a music teacher and he was going to teach her to play the piano. His name was Pastor Wilder. This was a good thing, and most of all, it kept her in church.

She informed me that finally she had started to play at her home church and looked forward to Sunday morning services every Sunday. It really made her day. Thank God her life had taken a turn for the better.

It was a good thing just to know that she was looking to the One that looked beyond her faults, and saw her needs. God is the only one that can do that. Through her faithfulness and devotion, many of her friends came to church to see what she was doing and stayed. They're there now, and I might add doing very well. Corine had a cousin named Edith. When she heard what was happening, she didn't believe it, and shocked her friends by showing up. To everyone's surprise she kept coming back. Finally she decided to join the church, and I'm told she's there now.

Favorite Scriptures

Psalm 37:1-7, New King James

Do not fret because of evildoers, nor be envious of the workers of iniquity. For they shall soon be cut down like the grass, and wither as the green herb. Trust in the Lord, and do good; dwell in the land, and feed on His faithfulness. Delight yourself also in the Lord, and He shall give you the desires of your heart. Commit your way to the Lord, trust also in Him, and He shall bring it to pass. He shall bring forth your righteousness as the light, and your justice as the noonday. Rest in the Lord, and wait patiently for Him; do not fret because of him who prospers in his way, because of the man who brings wicked schemes to pass.

Proverbs 4:1-7, New King James

*Hear my children, the instruction of a father,
And give attention to know understanding; for I give you good doctrine: do not forsake my law.
When I was my father's son, tender and the only one in the sight of my mother. He also taught me, and said to me: "let your heart retain my words; keep my commands, and live, get wisdom! Get understanding!
Do not forget, nor turn away from the words of my mouth. Do not forsake her, and she will preserve you; love her, and she will keep you. Wisdom is the principal thing; therefore get wisdom.*

19

Choices

Life is about choices. What a wonderful thing to change your life around, and live for the Lord; to do something good for yourself, and someone else. To make someone's day by doing them a favor, or say something nice for a change. Maybe give them a gift or even a smile. Remember if you really want to reap something good, you must sow something worthwhile. So many people don't realize this. Pray for someone. Tell them about the blessings and goodness of God. We need His guidance everyday regardless of circumstances. The effectual fervent prayer of a righteous man avail much. If there is something missing in your life, don't let it be the Lord. You will need Him now and always. When you consider the challenges, and opportunities that are offered in so many ways, we should enjoy sharing different beliefs, and ideas, instead of critical opinions.

Someone told me about a bad situation that turned out good. A guy named Bruce got married. Bruce had a very nice wife that was faithful, and true to him. He didn't appreciate it. He started running around, and hanging out in the street, and so did she. Bruce had grown up in church and knew better.

This meant that whatever he did, he always came back to the church, which was a good thing. His wife was named Sara. Sara was just the opposite of Bruce and did not grow up in a church going family. As a matter of fact she acted as if she had never heard the word prayer.

Bruce's friends went to a church that had a special Bible Study group. The participants were around his own age (about twenty one), so they could relate to each other. Sara was kind of violent, always fighting, carried a gun, and began to threaten Bruce for his behavior. This violent behavior never helps anything. They would fight all the time. A change had to come. Sara never knew how to behave as a wife him the beginning and Bruce was not doing what he knew. Sara had been married several times, and Bruce never knew this. He decided to end the marriage before he got in trouble. He and Sara got a divorce. He thanked God because a situation of this kind can never go on too long before something bad happens.

At this point, Bruce knew it was best to part ways before one would hurt the other. Bruce prayed and asked the Lord for guidance. About a year later Bruce met another lady in a restaurant, and started dating again. He had moved to another town, got a better job. Things were beginning to look up for him. With this great job, he could travel, and do all the nice things he wanted to do with his life.

Bruce began to tell his friends how happy he was, and how he was enjoying his life. He and his new friend Mindy started living together. He knew better. He realized from his study of the bible that this was wrong, but against his better judgment, he wanted to try living together again. It didn't work then and it wouldn't work now. Bruce found out what he already knew. Mindy wanted to get married and he wanted to wait. She asked for separate bedrooms, and began to make arrangements to move out of the house. Bruce got the message, and decided to marry her. About three months later, she became unfaithful and just wouldn't stay home.

Mindy came up pregnant with twin boys, and it didn't take long for Bruce to find out that this happened when she was in the streets. He started to leave her in the house, but he didn't want his friends to know that the children didn't belong to him. They would have teased him the rest of his life.

This was quite an ordeal for Bruce as he suffered the consequences. This situation caused Bruce to practice faithfulness even more, because the father of the twins had tried to separate them. His first instinct was to flee, and put it all behind him, and leave her and the kids, and never look back.

Bruce prayed and got stronger in the Lord. He was able to get through the ordeal by taking things one day at a time. Mindy too began to sense regret for her choices and she started seeking the Lord. The couple finally reconciled and got their lives together. Things began to look up for both of them. Bruce discovered that he actually was at the right place, at the right time. When Mindy began to live for the Lord she changed for the better and became an excellent wife and mother. They began attending church as a couple and Bruce was glad they stayed together. This ordeal caused Bruce and Mindy to develop a beautiful relationship with the Lord.

Whether you believe it or not discouragement is contagious and someone else can have an impact on your life decisions.

It's a blessing to pray for friends, and each other. It gives us the strength, that we need to get through each day, and so much can be accomplished together. When you express your true feelings, and deepest thoughts, it will become a reality.

This opens us up to a world of possibilities and acceptance. Especially, when we come to the realization that together we can do much more. Prayer is the key to unlocking so many doors that we normally wouldn't have access too. There is so much more to life, than what the natural world has to offer. Believe in the Lord and seek the things that are above.

I'm so glad that God's grace can fill a life with purpose and meaning, because whatever is said and done, He is in control, and will always be. If you don't have a favorite scripture, just browse through the bible. I know you will find one to your liking. Until then, start with the 23rd Psalm. Almost everybody knows that one or has heard it.

Look to the Lord, because His love will give you unending grace and mercy regardless of what's happening in your life. He is the source of all goodness. When you're concerned about potential outcome, trust Him and keep your mind on Him and He will keep you in perfect peace. He will also direct your path.

It's so great to have a prayer partner, someone who is committed to praying with you and for you on a regular basis. You will rest knowing that you're not alone because you have a faith filled partner.

When you're praying for family and friends, its important to give thanks to God. He will direct your path, guard your steps, and we will be inspired by every choice we make by His guidance.

Very few people want you to guide them because everyone wants to lead, and no one wants to follow. If you're serious about following the Lord, He will fill your life with purpose and meaning.

To be an example as a grateful Christian is a step in the right direction. We always want something from the Lord, and never thank Him for what He has already done, and what He will do.

There are times when we won't say thanks for anything, not even with the strength we possess, that He gives us to survive. He gave us life with divine wisdom and guidance. He is our comfort and help whatever the need may be. Let Him guide you, and you will never go wrong. Give your television a break. Read a scripture or as much as you can, and remember, God is whatever you need Him to be in your life.

It's a devastating experience when you feel that you have no hope whatsoever, but God loves you unconditionally, He is on your side because He cares. It's sad to forget to give thanks for health, peace of mind, and all the blessings that you enjoy in this life.

Just be grateful for what we have been given in the past, and appreciate what is yet to come, as He extends His blessings. You must know the prayer of the righteous avails much. Oftentimes, the more we receive we're still not content. Whatever possibilities come our way, come with a price because it's never enough. There is always stress to keep you company, and destroy any personal peace you might have. Meanwhile, that restless headache returns and that's something else to cause you to have a day that you're not looking forward to.

The Lord wants us to pursue peace for our own satisfaction and protection. He provides for us in His own way, and in His own time. The spiritual part of our lives is just as important if not more important than the other parts of our lives.

As we try to control our own life, the Lord gives us the knowledge of what should be done according to His will, and trying to please Him, by having Him in every aspect of your life. The experience of the Lord is an individual thing. You will certainly not be asked what someone else has been doing in their life, because He knows where every one lives, and what you have been doing all your life, and most of all. He will forgive you for your sins, if you ask Him.

There are statements made all the time. Why go to church? Sam or Bob goes, and they do things that I wouldn't dare to do. Why not go? You go everywhere else. It would help you, because it certainly will not hurt you.

When you need something, I mean really need a big favor, or something done immediately, it's usually, Lord have mercy, when something comes up, that we can't handle, when there's no solution to the matter, and we look for a quick fix. It's usually something that we need done in a hurry with no questions asked.

We call on the Lord because He can help, and won't tell anyone else. Unlike others, that doesn't have kindness in their vocabulary. It's good to do a little something to brighten another's day like an unexpected expression of concern—a card, a phone call, or maybe treating someone to lunch or dinner.

If you show love, when it's needed the most, I'm sure peace and joy will follow. If we're quiet and peaceful, when others mistreat, and persecute us, we demonstrate Christ-likeness. So many people react first, and think about control of the situation later. If you have a dear friend, try being one. It will help in the long run, or years to come, because a true friend in my estimation is one of life's choicest blessings.

Some people look at life and see only trouble, even though God's forgiveness and blessings are still yours for the asking. I guess it all depends on what you're looking for. You may begin a day, and think it will be great, only to find out you're being attacked by someone else, and their problems, that has absolutely nothing to do with you.

Thank God for restoring to us His power, guidance, and comfort in this life. We can worship Him publicly or privately in prayer wherever we are. Events in our life are hard to understand, and we know as time goes by, that God is completely still in control.

I've heard people say being a Christian takes all the fun out of life. Saying you can't do this or that, and they're still afraid to even try to attempt to experience a Christian life. How great and lavish God is. We're blessed with many thanks to Him. We cannot thank Him enough. We have absolutely no excuses for not doing the right thing at the right time. We have to look to Him anyway. Happiness is a surface emotion depending upon circumstances. When we have mood swings that are uncalled for, God remains the same. Satan is the one that is always planting doubt in your mind.

Eula Collier

Ecclesiastes 3, New King James

To everything there is a season, a time for every purpose under heaven: A time to be born, and a time to die; a time to plant, and a time to pluck what is planted; A time to kill, and a time to heal; a time to break down, and a time to build up; a time to weep, and a time to laugh; a time to mourn, and a time to dance; A time to cast away stones, and a time to gather stones; a time to embrace, and a time to refrain from embracing; A time to gain, and a time to lose; a time to keep, and a time to throw away; A time to tear, and a time to sew; a time to keep silence, and a time to speak; A time to love, and a time to hate; a time of war, and a time of peace. What profit has the worker from that in which he labors? I have seen the God-given task with which the sons of men are to be occupied. He has made everything beautiful in its time. Also He has put eternity in their hearts, except that no one can find out the work that God does from the beginning to end. I know that nothing is better for them than to rejoice, and to do good in their lives. And also that every man should eat and drink, and enjoy the good of all his labor—it is the gift of God. I know that whatever God does, it shall be forever. Nothing can be added to it. God does it, that men should fear before Him. That which is has already been, And what is to be has already been; And God requires an account of what is past. Moreover I saw under the sun; In the place of judgment, Wickedness was there; And in the place of righteousness, Iniquity was there. I said in my heart, "God shall judge the righteous and the wicked, for there is a time there for every purpose and for every work. I said in my heart concerning the condition of the sons of men, God tests them, that they may see that they themselves are like animals." For what happens to the sons of men also happens to animals; one thing befalls them: as one dies, so dies the other. Surely, they all have one breath; man has no advantage over animals, for all is vanity. All go to one place; all are from the dust, and all return to dust. Who knows the spirit of the sons of men, which goes upward, and the spirit of the animal, which goes down to the earth? So I perceived that nothing is better, than that a man should rejoice in his own works; for that is his heritage. For who can bring him to see what will happen after him?

20

Time: The Poem

Time is very important—it will not wait for you.

No matter where you go or what you do you should know the living God is with you. Just keep the faith and God will help you. As God go with you, be sure to go with God!

Everything is in His hands. You should keep all of His demands. Because time is not up to you—We never know how much time we have, until time for us is passed. We should always live as if every day would be our last, We have no power over time. Have patience, as well as faith, and wait. Sometimes it seems that the Lord might linger when you call—but He never comes late. Time is all we have, other than God, but you don't know how much time you do have.

Eula Collier

There is a right time for all things in our lives and there is safety in being in God's perfect timing. I pray you will be in God's perfect will with His perfect timing—not one step ahead or one step behind.

IT'S TIME!

21

Pictures

Pastor Barbara Winn

Pastor Barbara Winn

Grand opening Sunday

Rev. Barbara Winn, pastor of the Apostolic Faith Assembly, stands in the congregation's new building at 1823 7th St. NE. A grand opening for the facility, which seats 500, will be held Sunday at 11:10 a.m. The building, which costs about $500,000, also contains 10 classrooms and two offices. (Repository staff photo)

Pastor Barbara Winn

Pastor Barbara Winn

First Milburn Church and School for Black Children

Second Milburn School for Black Children

Milburn School for White Children

Milburn Community Entrance (first large bldg. is theater)

Milburn Tipple Dwelling Houses

Milburn Tipple and Coal Cars

Milburn Post Office and Clerk

Ambulance for Blacks

Resource

Thanks to Dale Payne, Author of *Pictorial History of Paint Creek 1750's-1950's* for the photos and historical information on Paint Creek.

About the Author

I grew up in West Virginia, graduated from Simmons High School in Montgomery and attended Bluefield State Teachers College. I am the mother of eight children and worked at Eastern Cloveridge.

In addition, I am the author of *The Three P's: Perseverance, Prison, and Pastor."* Down through the years, I have made some bad choices and mistakes, but I have always had what I needed, and some of the things I wanted, because God has always been on my side.